Strategic Studies Institute Monograph

RUSSIA IN THE ARCTIC

Stephen J. Blank

Editor

July 2011

*****

Published by Books Express Publishing
Books Express, 2011
ISBN 978-1-780395-16-6

Books Express publications are available from all good retail and online booksellers. For
publishing proposals and direct ordering please contact us at: info@books-express.com

CONTENTS

Foreword v

Introduction vii

1. Russia in the Arctic: Challenges to U.S. Energy
   and Geopolitics in the High North 1
   Ariel Cohen

2. The Arctic: A Clash of Interests or Clash of
   Ambitions 43
   Alexandr' Golts

3. Russian Military Presence in the High North:
   Projection of Power and Capacities
   of Action 63
   Marlène Laruelle

4. The Evolving Arctic Security Environment:
   An Assessment 91
   Katarzyna Zysk

About the Contributors 139

FOREWORD

This volume on the Arctic is the last volume in the set of five based on the Strategic Studies Institute (SSI)-U.S. State Department conference on Russia held in January 2010. The Arctic's importance to the United States and to the international community has grown by virtue of its enormous energy holdings and the prospect of increased year-round navigation due to climate change. Given its proximity to Russia and that country's dependence on energy for its economic growth and development, this area's importance to Russia has grown, leading Moscow to make aggressive claims on behalf of its Arctic interests.

Russia's claims have triggered considerable anxiety among other Arctic states. These considerations oblige analysts here and abroad to take regional developments in the Arctic quite seriously. Therefore, we are making these papers, which reflect Russian, American, and European analyses of the motives, capabilities, and interests of Russia in the Arctic, available to our readers so that they can benefit from the authors' expert insights.

DOUGLAS C. LOVELACE, JR.
Director
Strategic Studies Institute

INTRODUCTION

Due to changes in climate and technology, the Arctic Ocean is becoming increasingly navigable. Since potentially enormous energy holdings have been discovered there, and the Arctic constitutes Russia's northern coast, the area's commercial significance adds to its preexisting strategic importance for the Russian Federation. During the Cold War, the High North theater held acute strategic significance as the bastion for Russia's nuclear Northern Fleet. That significance, though diminished, still prevails. The Pacific side of the Arctic is becoming more important as China's power grows. The mounting importance of the area as a source of energy and trade for Russia merely adds to the Chinese factor. Bearing these points in mind, beginning in 2007 the Russian government has made a noisy and demonstrative effort to assert its claims in the Arctic but has also negotiated with other Arctic stakeholders, most prominently Norway, with whom it signed a treaty in 2010.

Given the growing strategic significance of the Arctic for Russia and other Arctic states like the United States, the Strategic Studies Institute added a panel on the Arctic to its January 2010 conference, "Contemporary issues in International Security," held at the Finnish embassy in Washington, DC. The papers in the present volume bring together Russian, European, and American analyses of the energy and military significance of the Arctic, a significance extending to the United States and other Arctic states, as well to Russia. These papers clarify the motives, stakes, and capabilities that Russia brings to the Arctic, thus their true importance lies in their implications for international security. Therefore they should help to advance our understanding of a region whose significance for the United States in terms of both energy and strategy will rise considerably in the foreseeable future.

CHAPTER 1

RUSSIA IN THE ARCTIC: CHALLENGES TO U.S. ENERGY AND GEOPOLITICS IN THE HIGH NORTH

Ariel Cohen

The Arctic has reemerged as a strategic area where vital U.S. interests are at stake. The geopolitical and geo-economic importance of the Arctic region is immense, as its mineral wealth is likely to turn the region into a booming economic frontier in the 21st century. The Arctic coasts and continental shelf are estimated to hold large deposits of oil, natural gas, methane hydrate (natural gas) clusters, and large quantities of valuable minerals.

With the shrinking of the polar ice cap, navigation through the Northwest Passage along the northern coast of North America may become increasingly possible with the help of icebreakers. Similarly, Russia is seeking to make the Northern Sea Route along the northern coast of Eurasia navigable for considerably longer periods during the year and is listing it as part of its *national* boundaries in the Kremlin's new Arctic strategy. Passage through these shorter routes will significantly cut the time and costs of shipping. (See Map 1-1.) In recent years, Russia has been particularly active in the Arctic, aggressively advancing its interests and claims by using international law and also establishing a comprehensive presence in the Arctic, including the projection of military might into the region.

1

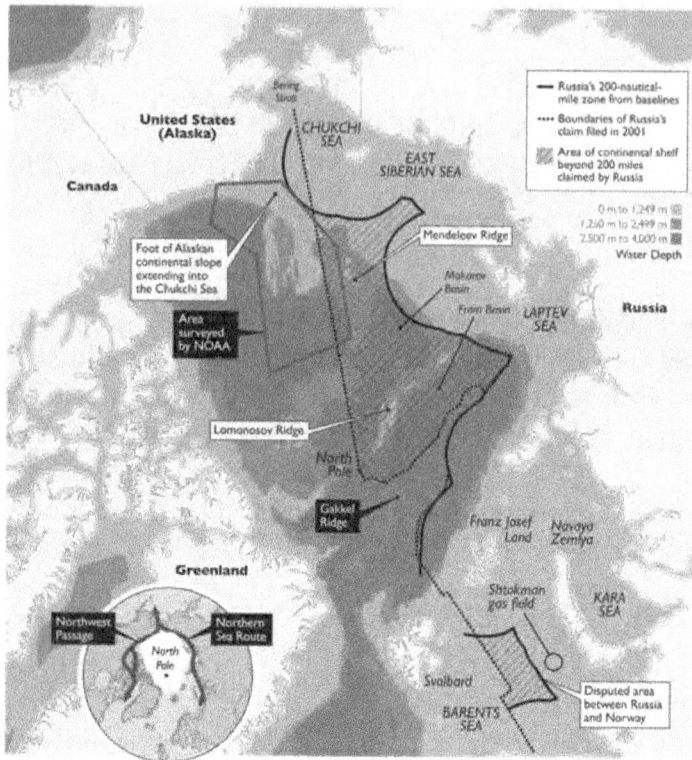

Source: Jeannette J. Lee, "New Seafloor Maps May Bolster U.S. Arctic Claims," *National Geographic News*, February 12, 2008, available from *news.nationalgeographic.com/news/2008/02/080212-AP-arctic-grab.html*.

Map 1-1. U.S. and Russian Interests in the Arctic.

Despite the Arctic's strategic location and vast resources, the United States has largely ignored this vital region. In the 11th hour of the Bush administration, however, the White House issued a new Arctic policy, but follow-through was left to the Obama administration, which has been slow to move on the issue. The United States needs to implement a comprehensive policy for the Arctic, including diplomatic, naval, military, and economic policy components. The United States needs to swiftly map U.S. territorial claims to determine their extent and to defend against claims by other countries. Thus exploiting the rich hydrocarbon resources in the Arctic will continue to remain relevant as China and India continue on courses of growth and global economies rebound. These resources have the potential to significantly enhance the economy and the energy security of North America and the world, and reduce U.S. dependence on Middle Eastern oil.

THE ARCTIC'S VAST UNTAPPED RESOURCES

The U.S. Geological Survey estimates that the Arctic might hold as much as 90 billion barrels of oil – 13 percent of the world's undiscovered oil reserves – and 47.3 trillion cubic meters (tcm) of natural gas – 30 percent of the world's undiscovered natural gas. At current consumption rates, assuming a 50 percent utilization rate of reserves, this is enough oil to meet global demand for 1.4 years and U.S. demand for 6 years. Arctic natural gas reserves may equal Russia's proven reserves, the world's largest.[1] (See Table 1-1.)

Area	Source	Total Oil	Total Natural Gas	World Oil	U.S. Oil	World Gas	U.S. Gas	World Gas Hydrate	U.S. Gas Hydrate
Arctic region	U.S. Geological Survey	90 bbo (estimated)	47 tcm (estimated)	1.4	6.0	8.0	36.0	-	-
Beaufort Sea	Canada Northwest Territories government	--	99 tcm (estimated)					17.0	76.0
Russian Federation (all territories)	U.S. Energy Information Agency	60 bbo (proven)	47.5 tcm (proven)	1.0	4.0	8.0	36.0	-	-
Russian Arctic Ocean territories	Russian government	3 bbo (proven); 67.7 bbo (estimated)	7.7 tcm (proven) 88.3 tcm (estimated)	1.1	5.0	16.0	73.5	-	-
Arctic territory claimed by Russia	Russian government	586 bbo	--	9.0	40.0				

Source: U.S. Geological Survey, U.S. Energy Information Agency, Government of the Northwest Territories of Canada and the Russian Federation.

Table 1-1. Estimated and Proven Oil and Natural Gas Reserves in the Arctic and Russia.

The Russian Ministry of Natural Resources estimates that the underwater Arctic region claimed by Russia could hold as much as 586 billion barrels of oil reserves.[2] The ministry estimates that proven oil deposits "in the Russian area of water proper" in the Barents, Pechora, Kara, East Siberian, Chukchi, and Laptev Seas could reach 418 million tons (3 billion barrels), and proven gas reserves could reach 7.7 tcm. Unexplored reserves could total 9.24 billion tons (67.7 billion barrels) of oil and 88.3 tcm of natural gas.[3] Overall, Russia estimates that these areas have up to 10 trillion tons of hydrocarbon deposits, the equivalent of 73 trillion barrels of oil.[4]

In addition to oil and gas, the Arctic seabed may contain significant deposits of valuable metals and precious stones, such as gold, silver, copper, iron, lead, manganese, nickel, platinum, tin, zinc, and diamonds. The rise of China, India, and other developing countries has increased global demand for these commodities.[5]

Alaska's North Slope.

Alaska's North Slope contributes significantly to U.S. oil production and could supply more. The North Slope is the region of Alaska extending from the Canadian border on the east to the Chukchi Sea Outer Continental Shelf (OCS) on the west. It includes the Chukchi Sea OCS, the Beaufort Sea OCS, the Arctic National Wildlife Refuge (ANWR), the Central Arctic (the region found between the Colville and Canning Rivers), and the National Petroleum Reserve Alaska.[6] (See Map 1-2.)

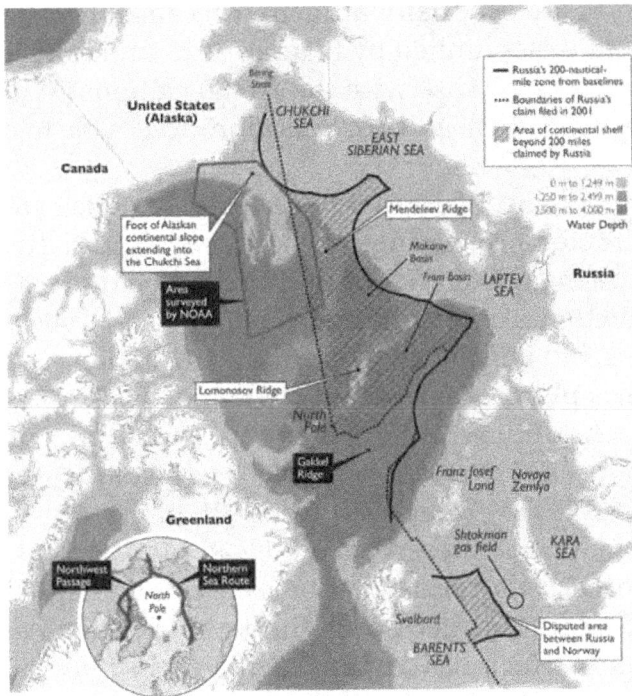

Source: Jeannette J. Lee, "New Seafloor Maps May Bolster U.S. Arctic Claims," *National Geographic News*, February 12, 2008, available from *news.nationalgeographic.com/news/2008/02/080212-AP-arctic-grab.html*.

Map 1-2. Alaska's North Slope.

Between 1977 and 2004, the Prudhoe Bay oil field on the North Slope produced more than 15 billion barrels of oil. By 1988, Prudhoe Bay accounted for more than 25 percent of U.S. crude oil production. However, the Prudhoe Bay oil field is currently in steep decline.[7] A U.S. Department of Energy report found that the Alaska North Slope has potentially 36 billion barrels of oil and 3.8 tcm of natural gas, close to Nigeria's proven reserves. The report also estimates that the Chukchi Sea OCS and the Beaufort Sea OCS hold combined energy reserves of 14 billion barrels of oil and about 2 tcm of natural gas.[8] Furthermore, these reserves are especially attractive because their development is less limited by federal, state, and local legislation, as is the case with the Arctic National Wildlife Refuge (ANWR), and are thus more accessible to drilling.

To enhance U.S. energy security, America should undertake a broad range of energy saving and diversification maneuvers, including expanding domestic oil production. America remains one of the largest producers, but it is the only oil-producing nation on earth that has placed a significant amount of its reserves out of reach. Until recently, potentially large U.S. natural gas deposits have been off limits. For instance, ANWR holds potential reserves of about 10 billion barrels of petroleum. Such reserves could lead to an additional 1 million barrels per day in domestic production. These could be transported south through the Trans-Alaska Pipeline, which has a spare capacity of 1 million barrels per day. An additional 1 million barrels per day would save the United States $123 billion in petroleum imports, create $7.7 billion in new economic activity, and generate 128,000 new jobs.[9]

Methane Hydrates.

Large methane hydrate deposits are located on the deep seabed of the Arctic Ocean.[10] Methane hydrates are a solid form of natural gas with 3,000 times the concentration of methane found in the atmosphere.[11] While no technology currently exists to mine methane clusters, the capability appears to be just over the horizon. The United States and Japan have agreed to cooperate in researching and developing commercial methane hydrate processing, with the goal of selling gas from methane hydrates by 2018.[12] The South Korean Ministry of Energy has also announced that it will work with the United States in exploring and developing methane hydrates deposits to develop a commercially viable energy source. Seoul, South Korea, is also hoping to participate in the U.S.-sponsored Alaska North Slope project in 2009 to test the viability of using methane hydrates as an energy source.[13]

Growing Importance of Arctic Energy.

Arctic oil and gas resources have become increasingly important, given the tight energy market. Escalating demand for energy in 2001-08, stagnating supply, political instability, growing resource nationalism, terrorism, and ethnic conflict combined to create a perfect storm in July 2008, with oil prices at $147 per barrel.[14] While oil prices later retreated to around $70-80 a barrel due to the financial crisis, global energy markets are expected to remain tight over the long term as the fundamentals remain largely the same, namely, rising demand from emerging markets outside U.S. control, and flattening supply. At the present writing, crude oil prices are reaching alarming heights once again, with prices around $114 a barrel. While these trends bode ill for security of energy supply, the resources in the Arctic offer a glimmer of hope.

U.S. Energy Supplies. Developing oil deposits in the Arctic is strategically important because the region is not beset by religious, ethnic, or social strife and resource nationalism that plague oil-producing countries in the Middle East, West Africa, and Latin America. One way to reduce U.S. dependency on foreign oil is to develop the Arctic oil fields. Such development would lower prices in the international oil market, even after accounting for high production costs and the time lag for bringing new oil fields online. Moreover, the rich oil and gas deposits in Alaska's North Slope and in the U.S. offshore Arctic territories could further increase U.S. energy supply by guaranteeing availability of additional domestic energy supplies in the time of a national emergency.[15]

Liquefied Natural Gas. U.S. demand for natural gas was growing up until the global financial crisis but has recently fallen. The Energy Information Administration (EIA) estimates that U.S. demand for natural gas fell by 1.5 percent in 2009 and will remain relatively unchanged during 2010.[16] Consumption is projected to rise slightly in 2011. Before the financial crisis, demand for natural gas was growing because U.S. energy demand has been growing; the current regulatory environment favors gas over coal and nuclear, creating numerous barriers to entry for building coal and nuclear plants. In addition, the relative importance of gas should grow in coming years if stricter climate regulations are enacted.

In 2004, then Chairman of the Federal Reserve Alan Greenspan saw increased imports of liquefied natural gas (LNG) as a "price-pressure safety valve" for reducing prices and filling the gap from the diminishing North American gas supply.[17] However, demand for LNG has been uneven in recent years and has also fallen due to the general drop in demand for gas and increased shale production.

However, natural gas demand will continue to grow in the years ahead, and increased imports of LNG would augment domestic production and increase competition. In 2008, Royal Dutch Shell's executive director of gas and power, Linda Cook, suggested that U.S. domestic production of natural gas could run 15–20 billion cubic feet per day below domestic demand by 2025.[18] This prediction was made before the augmented LNG production from the Arctic could help to meet future demand and to reduce gas prices in the domestic market, which would benefit industry and consumers.

Opening the Arctic Outer Continental Shelf.

Driven by escalating demand, the Mineral Management Service in the U.S. Department of Interior started offering oil and gas lease sales for drilling rights in the OCS in the Chukchi and Beaufort Seas in 2008. The Chukchi Sea lease sale in February 2008 was the first OCS lease sale in 17 years.[19]

International corporations began flocking to the High North. British Petroleum (BP) is developing a drilling project known as Liberty in the OCS. In February 2008, Royal Dutch Shell paid $2.1 billion for 275 lease blocks in the Chukchi Sea Lease Sale 193. At the February 2008 lease sale, Norway's StatoilHydro and Italy's ENI were the high bidders on a number of blocks. In total, seven companies participated in the Chukchi Sea lease sale, which spans an area covering 5,354 blocks.[20]

In October 2009, the Interior Department gave conditional approval to Royal Dutch Shell for exploration under two leases in the Beaufort Sea in Camden Bay, west of Kaktovik.[21] This exploration is opposed by environmental groups. In addition, Ken Salazar, Secretary of the Interior, conditionally approved Royal Dutch Shell's plan to drill three "exploratory," and "information-gathering" oil wells in the Chukchi Sea during the next open season, which will be from July to October 2010. This could open the door for offshore oil and gas production in a new region of the Arctic.

In a press release, Salazar stated that "a key component of reducing our country's dependence on foreign oil is the environmentally-responsible exploration and development of America's renewable and conventional resources." He continued, "By approving this Exploration Plan, we are taking a cautious but deliberate step toward developing additional information on the Chukchi Sea."[22]

These recent conditional approvals prompted Alaska Senator Lisa Murkowski, the ranking Republican on the Senate Energy and Natural Resources Committee, to say: "This is progress [representing] an encouraging sign that Alaska's oil and natural gas resources can continue to play a major role in America's energy security."[23]

In the future, these and other projects on the Arctic OCS could deliver gas to the lower 48 states via the Trans-Alaska Pipeline and the Canadian Mackenzie Valley Pipeline. These prospects began to look even brighter after a Canadian joint review panel endorsed the Mackenzie Valley pipeline.[24] The review panel is a government-appointed seven-member, independent body. There are still numerous obstacles to its realization, however. For example, the pipeline must receive support from indigenous people and other federal agencies. In addition, the pipeline is estimated to cost $16.2 billion, and with natural gas prices low, the project looks less favorable.

U.S. CLAIMS IN THE ARCTIC

The United States announced its new Arctic Region Policy on January 9, 2009, the 11th hour of the Bush Administration. The document is meant to serve as a strategic roadmap for more specific action plans. The policy states that the U.S. national and homeland security interests in the Arctic are missile defense and early warning; deployment of the sea and air systems for strategic sealift, strategic deterrence, maritime presence, and maritime security operations; ensuring freedom of navigation and airlift; and preventing terrorist attacks.[25] The document also delineates the U.S. position on international governance, boundary and transportation, economic issues and environment protection, and scientific cooperation.

The policy statement urges the U.S. Senate to approve the U.S. accession to the United Nations Convention on the Law of the Sea Treaty (UNCLOS) promptly. The United States currently is not a party to the UNCLOS and therefore is not bound by any procedures and determinations concluded through UNCLOS instruments. Instead, the United States is pursuing its claims "as an independent, sovereign nation," relying in part on Harry S. Truman's Presidential Proclamation No. 2667, which declares that any hydrocarbon or other resources discovered beneath the U.S. continental shelf are the property of the United States.[26] The United States can defend its rights and claims through bilateral negotiations and in multilateral venues such as the Arctic Ocean Conference in May 2008, which met in Ilulissat, Greenland.

11

Despite the new U.S. Arctic strategy, some have argued that the United States will not have leverage or a "seat at the table" to pursue or defend its Arctic claims if the United States is not a party to UNCLOS. However, U.S. attendance at the conference in Ilulissat as well U.S. participation in the Arctic Council[27] significantly weakened this argument. Even though the United States is not a party to UNCLOS, other Arctic nations "are unable to assert credible claims on U.S. territory in the Arctic or anywhere else in the world" because President Truman already underlined U.S. rights to Arctic resources with his proclamation.[28]

Yet to protect its rights, the United States needs to know how far its claims stretch into the Arctic Ocean. The new U.S. strategy urges the United States to take "all the actions necessary to establish the outer limit of the continental shelf appertaining to the United States."[29] The United States requires a modern flotilla of icebreakers to conduct mapping and to establish U.S. claims. Yet, a prominent Arctic expert argued before the U.S. Congress that the new policy does not outline funding allocations for acquisition of the new icebreakers.[30] The U.S. Coast Guard currently has only three icebreakers, of which only the *Healy* (commissioned in 2000) is relatively new. The other two icebreakers, while heavier than the *Healy* and thus capable of breaking through thicker ice, are at the end of their design service life after operating for about 30 years. Yet even if the United States begins allocating funds now, it will be 8 to 10 years before a new icebreaker can enter service. Moreover, no money has been allocated to build a new-generation heavy icebreaker.[31]

A 2008 mapping expedition undertaken by the icebreaker *Healy* in the Chukchi Sea focused on surveying an area 400 to 600 miles north of Alaska cost about

$1.2 million—a pittance compared to the billions of dollars of Arctic natural resources at stake. The survey indicated that the foot, or lowest part of the Alaskan continental shelf, stretches more than 100 miles beyond what was previously thought, thus expanding the U.S. claim.[32]

The United States has been mapping the bottom of the Arctic Ocean and the OCS since 2003.[33] Mapping is essential to determining the extent of the U.S. OCS and discovering whether the United States has any legitimate claims to territory beyond its 200-nautical-mile exclusive economic zone. According to the U.S. Department of State, the United States had made five Arctic cruises since 2003, and the Obama administration is continuing the multiyear effort to map the Arctic seabed.[34]

The United States and Canada have joined efforts in mapping missions to determine the boundary of each country's Arctic continental shelves.[35] The activities are part of the multiyear, multiagency effort undertaken by the U.S. Extended Continental Shelf Project, led by the Department of State, with vice co-chairs from the Department of the Interior and the National Oceanic Atmospheric Administration (NOAA). The joint 2009 continental Shelf Survey mission, which lasted from August 7 to September 16, 2009, marks the second year of such cooperative endeavors.[36] More such activities are planned for 2010.[37]

Mapping is important for resolving any conflicting claims by other Arctic nations. For example, the United States and Canada have likely claimed some of the same parts of the continental shelf.[38] Canada and Russia occupy 75 percent of the Arctic Ocean's coastline. They each claim that the channels between their Arctic islands and coasts are their "internal waters," and that if a foreign vessel needs to pass, it requires authorization. The position of the United States is that the Northern Sea Route and Northwest Passage are "international straits."[39] Mapping data will help to determine whether Russian claims conflict with U.S. and Canadian claims.

The presidential memorandum signed in January 2009 tasks the Department of Defense to "project a sovereign maritime presence" in the Arctic. In October 2009, the U.S. Navy released a Roadmap for Future Arctic Operations.[40] The objective of the roadmap is to ensure naval readiness and capability, and promote maritime security in the Arctic region. Essential elements of the plan include increasing operational experience, promoting cooperative partnerships, and improving environmental understanding.[41]

More recently, Senator Murkowski introduced Bill S.2849 to validate the U.S. interest in the Arctic. The bill requires a study and report on the feasibility of establishing a deep water sea port in the Arctic "to protect and advance strategic United States interests within the evolving and ever more important region."[42] The bill was referred to the Senate Armed Services Committee.[43]

RUSSIAN CLAIMS

After its invasion of Georgia, Russia has clearly hardened its international posture and is increasingly relying on power, not international law, to settle its claims. Moscow has also stepped up its anti-American policies and rhetoric and is likely to challenge U.S. interests whenever and wherever it can, including in the High North.

For over 2 centuries, Russia has taken its role as an Arctic power seriously. In 2001, Russia submitted to UNCLOS a formal claim for an area of 1.2 million square kilometers (460,000 square miles) that runs from the undersea Lomonosov Ridge and Mendeleev Ridge to the North Pole. This is roughly the combined area of Germany, France, and Italy.[44] The UN Commission refused to accept the claim, instead requesting "additional data and information."[45] Russia responded by sending a scientific mission including a nuclear-powered icebreaker and two mini-submarines to the area. During this meticulously organized media event, the mission planted the Russian flag on the ocean's floor at the Lomonosov Ridge after collecting soil samples that supposedly prove the ridge is part of the Eurasian landmass. During the mission, Deputy Chairman of the Russian Duma, Artur Chilingarov, the veteran Soviet explorer heading the scientific expedition, declared, "The Arctic is ours, and we should demonstrate our presence."[46] Such statements run counter to the spirit of international cooperation, striking as inappropriate for a scientific mission.

The United States has objected to these claims, stating that they have "major flaws." Professor Timo Koivurova of the University of Lapland in Finland stated that "oceanic ridges cannot be claimed as part of the state's continental shelf."[47] Russia planned to resubmit its claim in 2009, but missed the deadline. However, this does not mean that Moscow has been idle in its Nordic push. On the contrary, Russia has been moving rapidly to establish a comprehensive sea, ground, and air presence in the Arctic. Moscow has also released a new Arctic policy and has referenced the Arctic in several other important official publications. Despite missing the deadline, Russia is still pursuing its claims through UNCLOS. To advance these claims, Russia is currently undertaking a 3-year-long mapping mission of the Arctic.[48] This mission also has a peculiar military escort. Despite pursuing its claims through UNCLOS, Russia appears to be seeking to establish a comprehensive presence in the Arctic that will allow the Kremlin to take de facto possession of the underwater territories currently in dispute.

RUSSIA'S COMPREHENSIVE APPROACH TOWARD THE ARCTIC

In October 2009, Russian Prime Minister Vladimir Putin and, by extension, the Russian Federation, became head of the trustees of one of Russia's oldest institutions, the Russian Geographical Society.[49] Founded by Tsar Nicholas I in 1845 with headquarters in St. Petersburg, this prestigious society was started as part of the imperial drive for geographic expansion and exploration of the country's resources.[50] During his address to the society's congress, Putin praised the society's past contributions to Russia's geographic expansion and spoke about work ahead, including in the Arctic:

> When we say great, a great country, a great state— certainly, size matters. . . . When there is no size, there is no influence, no meaning. . . . The society can offer practical support to our plans to develop Eastern Siberia and the Far East, Yamal and the north of Krasnoyarsk region, to participate actively in further research projects in the Arctic and Antarctica, as well as environmental support of the Olympic Games in Sochi.[51]

While the society was funded by the state during Soviet times, it was left to fend for itself during the 1990s. But during his speech, Putin pledged funding for grants and promised to "do everything to help your work."[52] According to Vyacheslav Isayev, a member of the society's Sochi branch, the new president, the charter, and the creation of the board of trustees were all introduced in October 2009.[53]

Also during this time, Russian President Dmitry Medvedev signed a decree on October 21, 2009, creating a new Arctic university. The decree states that the State Technical University in Arkhangelsk will transform into the Northern (Arctic) Federal University.[54] As Arctic watcher Mia Bennett points out, it is likely that this institution will work to produce research supporting Russia's territorial claims, as well on oil and gas exploration prospects.[55]

Arctic Policy.

The two initiatives discussed above conform to policy objectives and directives dating back to July 2008. At that time, President Dmitry Medvedev published *The Foreign Policy Concept of the Russian Federation*.[56] This document established the importance of the Arctic in Russian national security policy: "In accordance with the international law, Russia intends to establish the boundaries of its continental shelf, thus expanding opportunities for exploration and exploitation of its mineral resources."[57]

Then, in September 2008, the Russian Federation approved its official Arctic strategy and published it in March 2009 under the subheading: "The fundamentals of state policy of the Russian Federation in the Arctic in the period up to 2020 and beyond."[58] The document clearly emphasizes the importance of the Arctic to Russia's economic and social development. In particular, the Arctic is seen as a key zone for expanding Russia's hydrocarbon reserves. According to a translation by the American Foreign Policy Council, the Russian Federation sees its "Arctic zone as a national strategic resource base capable of fulfilling the socio-economic tasks associated with national growth."[59]

Accordingly, one of the main goals of the Russian Federation's official state policy is to "expand the resource base of the Arctic zone of the Russian Federation, which is capable in large part of fulfilling Russia's needs for hydrocarbon resources, aqueous biological resources, and other forms of strategic raw material."[60] The main goal of the policy is to transform the Arctic into Russia's strategic resource base and make Russia a leading Arctic power by 2020. This is to be accomplished in stages. Cartographic, geological-geophysical, and hydrographic work must be carried out by 2010 to substantiate the outer boundary of Russia's Arctic zone. This data will support Russia's international claims. These claims and the codification of Russia's Arctic zone under international law, and the means for Russia's transportation of energy resources, must be realized before 2015. By 2020, the Arctic zone should be the leading strategic resource base of the country.

In order to realize these goals, the Russian Federation must provide for security. The main objectives of the Russian Federation's official state policy in the Arctic will be achieved by performing the following basic tasks:

> in the sphere of national security, the protection of the national border of the Russian Federation . . . it is necessary: to create general purpose military formations drawn from the Armed Forces of the Russian Federation, [as well as] other troops and military formations (most importantly, border units) in the Arctic zone of

the Russian Federation, capable of ensuring security under various military and political circumstances.[61]

The creation of this Arctic military group will be drawn from the armed forces of the Russian Federation as well as the power ministries (e.g., Federal Security Service [FSB] troops, border troops, and internal troops). Above all, the document calls for a coast guard that will patrol Russia's Arctic waters and estuaries.

Russian National Security Strategy.

On May 12, 2009, President Medvedev approved the *National Security Strategy of the Russian Federation until 2020* (NSS).[62] This doctrine replaced the national security concepts of 1997 and 2000. The document posited that Russia's ability to defend its national security depended overall on the country's economic potential. Russia's natural resources are viewed as a base for this economic development and determine its geopolitical influence. On February 4, 2009, Russian Prime Minister Vladimir Putin was quoted as saying: "Russia enjoys vast energy and mineral resources which serve as a base to develop its economy; as an instrument to implement domestic and foreign policy. The role of the country in international energy markets determines, in many ways, its geopolitical influence."[63]

As the late Roman Kupchinksy pointed out, the view that energy is a useful geopolitical tool would find its way into the new strategy. Paragraph 9 of the doctrine states: "The change from bloc confrontation to the principles of multi-vector diplomacy and the [natural] resources potential of Russia, along with the pragmatic policies of using them, has expanded the possibilities of the Russian Federation to strengthen its influence on the world arena."[64]

Perhaps more telling is paragraph 11, which lays out the future battlegrounds where conflicts over energy will occur: "The attention of international politics in the long term will be concentrated on controlling the sources of energy resources in the Middle East, on the shelf of the Barents Sea and other parts of the Arctic, in the Caspian Basin and in Central Asia." Ominously, the document posits that future competition for energy near Russian borders or its allies may be resolved with military force: "In case of a competitive struggle for resources it is not impossible to discount that it might be resolved by a decision to use military might. The existing balance of forces on the borders of the Russian Federation and its allies can be changed."[65]

This inclusion of armed conflict in the strategy document certainly got the attention of the Canadians. Rob Huebert, a political scientist of the University of Calgary's Center for Military and Strategic Studies, stated that the Russian outlook appears to be a "realistic" review of possible conflicts. He stated that the Russians have been talking very cooperatively, but they have been backing it up with an increasingly strong military set of options. This doctrine and Russia's aggressive behavior should spur Canada's efforts to beef up Arctic defenses, all the while continuing to look for areas of cooperation.[66]

The North Atlantic Treaty Organization (NATO) has also noticed the potential for conflict with Russia in the High North. Admiral James Stavridis, Supreme Allied Commander for Europe, speaking at the Royal United Services Institute in London on NATO's future direction, mentioned NATO-Russia relations in the context of territorial disputes and overlapping claims. He said:

This is something we are starting to spend more time looking at. I look at the High North and I think it could either be a zone of conflict, I hope not, a zone of competition, probably. It could also be cooperative . . . and as an alliance we should make this as cooperative as we possibly can.[67]

RUSSIA'S MILITARIZATION OF THE ARCTIC

As part of its effort to create a comprehensive presence in the Arctic, Russia has been steadily expanding its military component there since 2007. In August 2007, shortly after sending the scientific expedition to the Arctic ridge, then Russian President Putin ordered the resumption of regular air patrols over the Arctic Ocean. Strategic bombers, including the turboprop *Tupolev Tu-95*, supersonic bombers *Tu-160* (*Blackjack/ White Swan*) and *Tu-22M3* (*Backfire*), and the long-range anti-submarine warfare patrol aircraft Tu-142 have flown patrols since then.[68] According to the Russian Air Force, the Tu-95 bombers refueled in flight to extend their operational patrol area.[69] During 2007 alone, Russian bombers penetrated the North American Aerospace Defense Command (NORAD) 12-mile air defense identification zone surrounding Alaska 18 times.[70] Since August 2007, the Russian Air Force has flown more than 90 missions over the Arctic, Atlantic, and Pacific Oceans.[71]

On the strategic level, the Russian Navy is expanding its presence in the Arctic for the first time since the end of the Cold War.[72] Lieutenant General Vladimir Shamanov, head of the Defense Ministry's combat training department, said that the Russian Navy is increasing the operational radius of the Northern Fleet's submarines and that Russia's military strategy might be reoriented to meet threats to the country's interests in the Arctic, particularly with regard to its continental shelf. Shamanov said that "we have a number of highly professional military units in the Leningrad, Siberian and Far Eastern military districts, which are specifically trained for combat in Arctic regions."[73]

On July 14, 2008, the Russian Navy announced that its fleet had "resumed a warship presence in the Arctic." These Arctic naval patrols include the area of the Spitsbergen archipelago that belongs to Norway, a NATO member. Russia refuses to recognize Norway's right to a 200-nautical-mile exclusive economic zone around Spitsbergen. Russia deployed an anti-submarine warfare (ASW) destroyer followed by a guided-missile cruiser armed with 16 long-range anti-ship cruise missiles designed to destroy aircraft carriers.[74]

The resumption of Cold War–style patrols and increased naval presence in the Arctic is in keeping with Moscow's more forward posture and is intended to increase its leverage vis-à-vis territorial claims. Moscow is taking the dual approach of projecting military power while invoking international law. Regarding the naval deployments near Spitsbergen, the Russian Navy stated: "Sorties of warships of the Northern Fleet will be made periodically with a necessary regularity. All actions of the Russian warships are fulfilled strictly in accordance with the international maritime law, including the UN Convention on the Law of the Sea."[75]

At a meeting of the Russian government's Maritime Board in April 2008, Russian Foreign Minister Sergei Lavrov backed a policy of settling territorial disputes in the region with the countries bordering the Arctic through cooperation. Then-First Deputy Prime Minister Sergei Ivanov stressed in his remarks that Russia observes international law on the matter through adherence to two international conventions: the 1958 Convention on the Continental Shelf, signed by Canada, Denmark, Norway, Russia, and the United States; and the 1982 UNCLOS.[76]

While paying lip service to international law, Russian's ambitious actions hearken back to 19th century statecraft rather than the 21st century law-based policy. They appear to indicate that the Kremlin believes that credible displays of power will settle the conflicting territorial claims. By comparison, the West's posture toward the Arctic has been irresolute and inadequate.

During 2008 and 2009, Russian icebreakers were constantly patrolling in the Arctic. Russia has the largest such flotilla in the world: 18 operational icebreakers.[77] Seven of these are nuclear, including the *50 Years of Victory*, the largest icebreaker in the world.[78] Russia is modernizing its Northern Fleet and hopes to expand funding for more nuclear icebreakers.

Indeed, Russia plans to build new nuclear-powered icebreakers starting in 2015. In April 2009, Segey Kirienko, director of Rosatom State Corporation, announced that government funding for new nuclear icebreakers in the federal budget would total U.S. $57 million; and another U.S. $150 million for 2010-11. Experts estimate that Russia will need to build six to 10 nuclear icebreakers over the next 20 years to maintain and expand its current level of operations.[79]

RUSSIAN COMMERCIAL ACTIVITY

Shortly after the release of the Arctic strategy in August 2008, President Medvedev signed into force a law that allows "the government to allocate strategic oil and gas deposits on the continental shelf without auctions." The law restricts participation to companies with 5 years' experience in a region's continental shelf and in which the government controls no less than a 50 percent stake, thus effectively allowing only state-controlled Gazprom and Rosneft to participate.[80]

After the global financial crisis ensued and Russia entered a deep recession in 2008, the Kremlin back-tracked on this policy and began seeking foreign investors for Arctic gas development. In September 2009, Prime Minister Putin hosted numerous oil and gas executives from around the world in Salekhard, Siberia, to discuss the development of liquefied natural gas on the Yamal peninsula in the Arctic.[81] Russia badly needs the foreign investment, as well as the technical expertise which the international oil companies have.

In addition to icebreakers, Russia is constructing an Arctic oil rig in the northern shipbuilding center of Severodvinsk, scheduled for completion by the summer of 2010 and to be handed over to Gazprom.[82] The rig is to be the first of its kind, capable of operating in temperatures as low as minus 50 degrees Celsius (minus 58 degrees Fahrenheit) and withstanding the impact of ice packs. The new rig was commissioned by the state-owned Gazprom, demonstrating that Russia is serious about oil exploration in the Arctic.[83]

Russia announced plans in May 2008 for a fleet of floating and submersible nuclear power stations for use in exploiting Arctic oil and gas. Construction of the prototype station, Akademik Lomonosov, was scheduled to be completed at Baltiysky Zavod in St. Petersburg[84] by the end of 2010.[85] It will be deployed at Vilyuchinsk, in the Kamchatka region in Russia's Far East by the end of 2012.[86] A floating power plant has a higher risk of accident with potential disastrous impact on the environment.[87] Rosatom plans to construct seven more floating nuclear power plants to be used on the Kola, Yamal, and Chukotka peninsulas and the Kamchatka region. Further sites for floating nuclear plants include Yakutia and Taimyr.[88]

ARCTIC SEA LANES

The Arctic Ocean has two main sea routes that are open to shipping for about 5 months per year with the help of icebreakers: the Northern Sea Route and the Northwest Passage. (See Map 1.) The Northern Sea Route links the Barents Sea in the west with the Chukchi Sea to the east and services isolated settlements along Russia's long Arctic coastline. If the Arctic ice cap continues to shrink, the northern route will become a major conduit for international shipping.[89] If the Northern Sea Route is navigable for a longer period of time, it would make the transportation of commodities to international markets easier and may significantly reduce transportation costs between the Pacific Rim and Northern Europe and Eurasia.

A Russian Information Agency *Novosti* political commentator argued:

> The country that dominates this sea lane will dictate its terms to the developers of the shelf deposits and will see the biggest gains from the transportation of raw materials to the Pacific and the Atlantic. These include billions of tons of oil and trillions of cubic meters of gas, not to mention other minerals in which the local lands abound.[90]

Another Russian expert similarly warned, "If we do not start immediately reviving the Arctic transportation system, voyages on the Northern Sea Route will be led by the Japanese or the Americans."[91]

To protect critical lines of transportation such as the Northern Sea Route, and to secure Russian Federation national borders, Russia is planning to conduct a military buildup in the Arctic. According to Marcel de Haas, Senior Research Fellow at the Netherlands Institute of International Relations Clingendael, General Nikolay Patrushev in 2004, at the time head of the FSB (successor to the domestic wing of the KGB), a Putin confidant, and today Secretary of the Russian National Security Council, created a special Arctic Directorate at the FSB.[92]

Russia's new Arctic policy, according to de Haas, emphasizes FSB elements more than Ministry of Defense units, stating that the FSB will provide a system of coastal defense.[93] This system will augment the FSB-controlled border troops and will patrol Russia's Arctic borders.[94] This will ultimately require the creation of more border infrastructure and equipping of the coast guard force with the necessary equipment to enable it to control and monitor Russia's Arctic zone. According to Roger McDermott, while the FSB will take the lead on the coastal defense, a military assault force could be airlifted into the area.[95]

The Russian Federation Arctic policy proclaims that "the use of the Northern Sea Route as a national unified transportation link of the Russian Federation in the Arctic"[96] to be a national interest of Russia.[97] In November 2009, Russia announced that it will charge ships a "fair" price to take the Northern Sea Route between the Atlantic to the Pacific. This route, which is already used by Rosneft, is three times faster than its alternative through the Suez canal. Alexasandr Davydenko, head of the Federal Sea and River Transport Agency, said in an interview for *Russia Today* that he hopes the ice will melt soon.[98] But the capabilities of

Russian ports are not adequate to receive more ships. The port of Murmansk already tenders the construction of new terminals to foreign bidders.[99]

The United States, on the other hand, stated in its Arctic Strategy that:

> Freedom of the seas is a top national priority. Northern Sea Route includes straits used for international navigation; the regime of transit passage applies to passage through those straits. Preserving the rights and duties relating to navigation and overflight in the Arctic region supports our ability to exercise these rights throughout the world, including through strategic straits.[100]

The Northwest Passage.

The Northwest Passage runs through Canada's Arctic archipelago. If the polar ice cap continues to recede, the Northwest Passage will become a major shipping lane for international trade between Europe and Asia, cutting transit times substantially. Currently, navigation is possible along the Northwest Passage during a 7-week period with the use of icebreakers.[101]

According to a report by the U.S. Office of Naval Research, by 2050 "[t]he Northwest Passage through the Canadian Archipelago and along the coast of Alaska will be ice-free and navigable every summer by non-icebreaking ships."[102] Use of the Northwest Passage is a contentious issue between the United States and Canada. The United States argues that "it is a strait for international navigation," regarding the Northwest Passage as international waters. Canada, on the other hand, claims that the straits of the sea route are "inland seas" falling under Canadian sovereignty.[103] After a 1985 incident in which a U.S. Coast Guard icebreaker passed through the waters without asking for Canadian permission, Canada declared the Northwest Passage to be "internal waters." On December 3, 2009, the Canadian House of Commons renamed the Northwest Passage the "Canadian Northwest Passage."[104] Resolving this dispute amicably is essential so that both countries can benefit from further economic and security cooperation.

INTERNATIONAL COOPERATION

The United States has a strong interest in cooperating with its Arctic neighbors, especially Canada, in developing offshore oil and gas fields and policing the region. Canada is a close NATO ally and a reliable oil and natural gas supplier to the United States. Canada also maintains a very friendly investment climate compared to other energy-producing nations.

At a recent conference, Robert McLeod, former minister of energy of Canada's Northwest Territories, said that exploitation of the oil and gas resources in the Arctic would improve North American energy security and that "the combined northern gas reserves in Canada and the United States could supply southern markets in Canada and the United States with 8 billion cubic feet per day."[105]

Opportunities also exist for cooperation in defense and national security. As during the Cold War, the United States could work with its NATO partners in the Arctic region. This is already taking place at the U.S. Air Force base in Thule, Greenland, under bilateral agreements between the United States and Denmark that facilitate this cooperation. The United States and Canadian Coast Guards resupply Thule Air Base.[106] The most important example of U.S.–Canadian defense cooperation is North American Aerospace

Defense Command (NORAD). The Alaskan NORAD Region is regaining its former relevance as the Russian bombers resumed their incursions.[107]

Warmer ocean temperatures and a smaller ice cap would provide increased opportunities for U.S.-Canadian maritime cooperation in combating potential terrorist operations and unlawful navigation. Moreover, warming of the northern portion of the Bering Sea may induce the migration of fish to the Arctic Ocean, creating the necessity for joint fishing regulation.[108] With the North Pacific already suffering from massive poaching, unlawful fishing could become a problem. Joint law enforcement coordination for commercial fishing will be increasingly important.

REESTABLISHING THE U.S. ARCTIC PRESENCE

The United States needs to revitalize its Arctic policy, beginning by elevating U.S. Arctic policy from its third-tier status to a national priority. Specifically, the United States should:

- **Create an interagency task force on the Arctic** at the NSC level, bringing together the Departments of Defense, State, Interior, and Energy to develop the overall U.S. policy toward the region. The United States should use diplomatic, military, and economic means to maintain its sovereign rights in the Arctic. The United States should also establish a Joint Task Force–Arctic Region Command, headed by a Coast Guard flag officer. This joint task force would maintain U.S. sovereign rights and have an interagency staff with representatives from relevant U.S. agencies and departments. The United States should also establish an Arctic Coast Guard Forum modeled after the highly successful Northern Pacific Coast Guard Forum.

- **Accelerate the acquisition of icebreakers** to support the timely mapping of the Arctic OCS and the Arctic in general to advance U.S. national interests. The United States needs to swiftly map U.S. claims on the OCS and areas adjacent to Alaska to preserve its sovereign territorial rights. Timely mapping will be important as the other Arctic nations submit their claims within the 10-year window. The United States should not rely on mapping from other countries to advance its claims or to defend against the claims of other countries.

- **Provide the U.S. Coast Guard with a sufficient operations and maintenance budget** to support an increased, regular, and influential presence in the Arctic.

- **Reach out to Canada, Norway, Denmark, and, wherever possible, Russia.** Coordination, cooperation, and diplomacy with Canada and European allies with interests in the region will be required to prevent conflict with Russia and to maintain the special relationship with Canada. The United States needs to work with Canada to develop a mutually beneficial framework for settling outstanding legal issues and the commercial exploitation of Arctic hydrocarbons.

- **Create a public–private Arctic task force** to provide a formal avenue for the private sector to advise the U.S. Government on Arctic economic development. This task force should include representatives from energy, natural resources, and shipping sectors among others.

- **Authorize oil exploration and production in ANWR and other promising Arctic areas** in order to expand domestic energy supply. Congress should also streamline regulations for areas that it has already opened but heavily regulated.

CONCLUSION

As an Arctic nation, the United States has significant geopolitical and geo-economic interests in the High North. The United States should not just have a place at the table, but also seek to lead in navigating the nascent challenges and opportunities, such as disputes over the Outer Continental Shelf, the navigation of Arctic sea-lanes, and commercial development of natural resources and fisheries. The United States needs to revitalize its Arctic policy and commit the necessary resources to sustain America's leadership role in the High North.

ENDNOTES - CHAPTER 1

1. Jad Mouawad, "Oil Survey Says Arctic Has Riches," *The New York Times*, July 24, 2008, available from *www.nytimes.com/2008/07/24/business/24arctic.html*; and Joe Carroll, "Arctic May Hold 90 Billion Barrels of Oil, U.S. Says," *Bloomberg.com*, July 23, 2008, available from *www.bloomberg.com/apps/news?pid=20601082*.

2. Scott G. Borgerson, "Arctic Meltdown," *Foreign Affairs*, March/April 2008, available from *www.foreignaffairs.org/20080301faessay87206/scott-g-borgerson/arctic-meltdown.html*.

3. Mikhail Krutikhin, "Arctic Ocean Prospects," *Kommersant*, May 30, 2008, available from *www.kommersant.com/p897663/Expert_shares_his_view_of_possible_oil_mining_in_the_Arctic_zone*.

4. Richard A. Lovett, "Russia's Arctic Claim Backed by Rocks, Officials Say," *National Geographic News,* September 21, 2007, available from *news.nationalgeographic.com/news/pf/47871933.html.*

5. Kevin Krajick, "Race to Plumb the Frigid Depths," *Science,* Vol. 315, No. 5818, March 16, 2007, pp. 1525–1528; and Borgerson, "Arctic Meltdown."

6. National Energy Technology Laboratory, *Alaska North Slope Oil and Gas: A Promising Future or an Area in Decline?* Washington, DC: U.S. Department of Energy, August 2007, pp. vii, available from *www.netl.doe.gov/technologies/oil-gas/publications/EPreports /ANSFullReportFinalAugust2007.pdf.* The only part of the Arctic National Wildlife Refuge (ANWR) where oil and gas prospecting and future production might take place, pending a decision by Congress, is the refuge's 1002 Area due to its potentially huge oil and gas deposits. The ANWR 1002 Area comprises 1.5 million acres of coastal plain. Oil and gas production in any part of the Arctic National Wildlife Refuge can take place only when "authorized by an act of Congress." See U.S. Geological Survey, *Arctic National Wildlife Refuge, 1002 Area, Petroleum Assessment, 1998, Including Economic Analysis,* April 2001, available from *pubs. usgs.gov/fs/fs-0028-01/fs-0028-01.pdf;* U.S. Fish & Wildlife Service, "Management of the 1002 Area within the Arctic Refuge Coastal Plain," *Arctic National Wildlife Refuge,* September 12, 2008, available from *arctic.fws.gov/1002man.htm.*

7. U.S. Department of Energy, *Alaska North Slope Oil and Gas,* p. vii.

8. *Ibid.,* pp. vii-viii. The Department of Energy's report estimates that the Chukchi Sea OCS has 10 billion barrels of oil and 1.4 trillion cubic meters (tcm) of natural gas and that the Beaufort Sea OCS has 4 billion barrels of oil and 0.57 tcm of gas. Nigeria's proved oil reserves are over 37 billion barrels. See "Rank Order-Oil," Washington, DC: Central Intelligence Agency, *The World Factbook,* June 19, 2008, available from *www.cia.gov/library/publications/the-world-factbook/rankorder/2179rank.html;* "Rank Order-Natural gas-proved reserves," *The World Factbook,* Washington, DC: Central Intelligence Agency, June 19, 2008, available from *www. cia.gov/library/publications/the-world-factbook/rankorder/2179rank. html.*

9. David W. Kreutzer, "The Economic Case for Drilling Oil Reserves," Heritage Foundation WebMemo No. 2093, October 1, 2008, available from *www.heritage.org/Research/EnergyandEnvironment/wm2093.cfm*. Potential oil reserves in the ANWR can be considerable. A U.S. Geological Survey report in 1998, updated in 2001, was based on "3 years of study" in the ANWR 1002 Area alone where "new field studies were conducted, new well and sample data were analyzed, and new geophysical data were acquired." The estimated reserves of technically recoverable oil range from 5.7 billion to 16 billion barrels in all of the ANWR 1002 Area, "with a mean value of 10.4 billion barrels." U.S. Geological Survey, Arctic National Wildlife Refuge, 1002 Area, Petroleum Assessment, 1998, Including Economic Analysis.

10. Krajick, "Race to Plumb the Frigid Depths."

11. Federal Institute for Geosciences and Natural Resources, "Arctic," updated October 18, 2004, available from *www.bgr.de/ecord/index.html?/ecord/polar_oceans/arctic_ocean.htm*; Michael D. Max, Jürgen Mienert, Karin Andreassen, and Christian Berndt, "Gas Hydrate in the Arctic and Northern North Atlantic Oceans," in Michael D. Max, ed., *Natural Gas Hydrate in Oceanic and Permafrost Environments*, Dordrecht, The Netherlands: Kluwer Academic Publishers, 2003, pp. 175-176, 178, 180-182; N. N. Lebedeva-Ivanova and D. G. Gee, "Crustal Structure of the Podvodnikov Basin," *Geophysical Research Abstracts*, Vol. 7, 2005.

12. "US and Japan Agree to Joint Methane Hydrate Study," *Alexander's Gas & Oil Connections*, June 16, 2008, available from *www.gasandoil.com/goc/news/ntn82505.htm*.

13. "South Korea and US Warm to Gas Hydrates," *Alexander's Gas & Oil Connections*, May 15, 2008, available from *www.gasandoil.com/goc/news/ntn82082.htm*.

14. Ariel Cohen and Owen Graham, "What Is Driving the High Oil Prices?" June 9, 2008, Heritage Foundation *WebMemo* No. 1951, available from *www.heritage.org/Research/EnergyandEnvironment/wm1951.cfm*.

15. Paul Ziff, "Cross-Border Regulatory Collaboration in Its Context: Energy Balances and Energy Policy," Washington, DC:

Woodrow Wilson International Center for Scholars, Canada Institute, *One Issue, Two Voices* No. 2, September 2004, p. 12, available from *www.wilsoncenter.org/topics/pubs/ACF1D90.pdf*.

16. *Short-Term Energy Outlook*, Energy Information Agency, January 12, 2010, available from *www.eia.doe.gov/emeu/steo/pub/contents.html*.

17. Ann Davis and Russell Gold, "Surge in Natural-Gas Price Stoked by New Global Trade," *The Wall Street Journal*, April 18, 2008, p. A1.

18. *Ibid.*

19. "MMS Calls for Information and Nominations of Next Arctic Lease Sale," *Alexander's Gas & Oil Connections*, September 25, 2007, available from *www.gasandoil.com/goc/news/ntn73932.htm*; and "Alaskan Oil and Gas Blocks for Sale," *Alexander's Gas & Oil Connections*, February 4, 2008, available from *www.gasandoil.com/goc/news/ntn80617.htm*.

20. "Shell Bids for 275 Blocks Offshore Alaska," *Alexander's Gas & Oil Connections*, March 4, 2008, available from *www.gasandoil.com/goc/company/cnn81088.htm*; "StatoilHydro High Bidder on 16 Leases in Alaska Lease Sale," *Alexander's Gas & Oil Connections*, March 4, 2008, available from *www.gasandoil.com/goc/company/cnn81086.htm*; and "ENI Wins 18 Exploration Blocks in Alaskan Lease Sale," *Alexander's Gas & Oil Connections*, March 4, 2008, available from *www.gasandoil.com/goc/company/cnn81084.htm*.

21. Erika Bolstad, "Interior OKs exploratory drilling by Shell in Chukchi Sea," *Anchorage Daily News*, December 7, 2009, available from *www.adn.com/1536/story/1044468.html*.

22. Available from *www.mms.gov/alaska/latenews/newsrel/2009 nr/2009_1207.pdf*.

23. "Interior OKs exploratory drilling by Shell in Chukchi Sea," December 7, 2009, available from *www.adn.com/2009/12/07/1044468/interior-oks-exploratory-drilling.html#ixzz1IJ5b7UR0*.

24. Available from *arctic.foreignpolicyblogs.com/2010/01/02/canadian-federal-govt-endorses-mackenzie-valley-pipeline/*.

25. Available from *www.fas.org/irp/offdocs/nspd/nspd-66.htm*.

26. Steve Groves, "LOST in the Arctic: The U.S. Need Not Ratify the Law of the Sea Treaty to Get a Seat at the Table," Heritage Foundation *WebMemo* No. 1957, June 16, 2008, available from *www.heritage.org/Research/InternationalLaw/wm1957.cfm*; and Harry S. Truman, "Policy of the United States with Respect to the Natural Resources of the Subsoil and Sea Bed of the Continental Shelf," Presidential Proclamation No. 2667, September 28, 1945, available from *www.presidency.ucsb.edu/ws/index.php?pid=12332*.

27. Available from *arctic-council.org/section/the_arctic_council*.

28. Groves, "LOST in the Arctic."

29. Available from *www.fas.org/irp/offdocs/nspd/nspd-66.htm*.

30. Statement of Scott G. Borgerson, visiting Fellow for Ocean Governance at the Council on Foreign Relations, before the Committee on Foreign Relations, U.S. Senate, Washington DC, May 5, 2009.

31. Amy McCullough, "Coast Guard Gets $30M to Overhaul Icebreaker," *Navy Times*, October 17, 2008, available from *www.navytimes.com/news/2008/10/cg_polarstar_101608w*; National Research Council of the National Academies, *Polar Icebreakers in a Changing World: An Assessment of U.S. Needs*, Washington, DC: The National Academies Press, 2007, p. 15; Borgerson, "Arctic Meltdown"; and Sandi Doughton, "Aging Fleet Slows U.S. in Arctic 'Chess Game'," *The Seattle Times*, September 20, 2007, available from *seattletimes.nwsource.com/html/localnews/2003893175_icebreakers20m.html*.

32. *Ibid.*; and Nicholas Kralev, "U.S. Pursues Arctic Claim," *The Washington Times*, May 13, 2008, available from *www.washingtontimes.com/news/2008/may/13/us-pursues-arctic-claim*.

33. Krajick, "Race to Plumb the Frigid Depths"; U.S. State Department, "Defining the Limits of the U.S. Continental Shelf," available from *www.state.gov/g/oes/continentalshelf*.

34. Lauren Morello, "U.S. pushes for Law of the Sea ratification as new Arctic mapping project begins," *New York Times*, July 29, 2009, available from *www.eenews.net/public/climatewire/2009/07/29/1*.

35. "Russians to dive below the North Pole," *BBC News*, July 24, 2007, available from *http://news.bbc.co.uk/2/hi/europe/6914178.stm*

36. Available from *continentalshelf.gov/*.

37. "Scientists collaborate in exploring continent's extended continental shelf," *Media Newswire*, September 17, 2009.

38. Jeannette J. Lee, "New Seafloor Maps May Bolster U.S. Arctic Claims," *National Geographic News*, February 12, 2008, available from *news.nationalgeographic.com/news/2008/02/080212-AP-arctic-grab.html*.

39. Lee-Anne Goodman, "Arctic a growing security issue for U.S.: CIA shares spy photos of ice cap," *Winnipeg Free Press*, January 10, 2010.

40. Available from *www.wired.com/images_blogs/dangerroom/2009/11/us-navy-arctic-roadmap-nov-2009.pdf*.

41. *Ibid.*

42. Available from *www.opencongress.org/bill/111-s2849/show*.

43. *Ibid.*; and *arctic.foreignpolicyblogs.com/2009/12/09/senator-murkowski-introduces-bill-on-alaskan-deep-water-port/*.

44. Dave Sloggett, "Climate Change Offers Planners New Horizons," *Jane's Defence Weekly*, August 22, 2007, p. 23; and Lovett, "Russia's Arctic Claim Backed by Rocks, Officials Say."

45. Commission on the Limits of the Continental Shelf, "Outer Limits of the Continental Shelf Beyond 200 Nautical Miles from the Baselines," UN Office of Legal Affairs, Division for Ocean Affairs and the Law of the Sea, updated November 15, 2004, available from *www.un.org/depts/los/clcs_new/submissions_files/submission_rus.htm*.

46. Robert Amsterdam, "The Arctic Claim," August 3, 2007, available from *www.robertamsterdam.com/2007/08/the_arctic_claim. htm*; Max Delany, "Gas and Glory Fuel Race for the North Pole," *The St. Petersburg Times*, July 31, 2007, available from *www.sptimes-russia.com/index.php?action_id=2&story_id=22491*.

47. Kralev, "U.S. Pursues Arctic Claim."

48. John Vinocur, "A Heads-Up on Russia's Role in Arctic," December 7, 2009, available from *www.nytimes.com/2009/12/08/world/europe/08iht-politicus.html*.

49. Maria Antonova, "State Lays Claim to Academic Society," *Moscow Times*, November 19, 2009, available from *www.themoscowtimes.com/news/article/state-lays-claim-to-academic-society/389895.html*.

50. *Ibid.*

51. *Ibid.*

52. *Ibid.*

53. *Ibid.*

54. Available from *arctic.foreignpolicyblogs.com/2009/11/07/new-arctic-university-to-open-in-russia/*.

55. *Ibid.*

56. Dmitry Medvedev, "The Foreign Policy Concept of the Russian Federation," Executive Office of the President of the Russian Federation, July 12, 2008, available from *www.kremlin.ru/eng/text/docs/2008/07/204750.shtml*.

57. Office of the President, Official Web Portal, "The Foreign Policy Concept of the Russian Federation," July 12, 2008, available from *archive.kremlin.ru/eng/text/docs/2008/07/204750.shtml*.

58. "The fundamentals of state policy of the Russian Federation in the Arctic in the period up to 2020 and beyond," September 2008, available from *www.scrf.gov.ru/documents/98.html*.

59. Ilan Berman, ed.,"Russia's New Arctic Strategy," *Russia Reform Monitor*, American Foreign Policy Council, May 4, 2009, available from *www.afpc.org/publication_listings/viewBulletin/647*.

60. *Ibid.*

61. *Ibid.*

62. "Strategy and the National Security of the Russian Federation until 2020," No. 537, May 12, 2009, available from *www.scrf. gov.ru/documents/99.html*.

63. Roman Kupchinsky, "Energy and the Russian National Security Strategy," Jamestown Foundation, *Eurasia Daily Monitor*, Vol. 6, Issue 95, May 18, 2009, available from *www.jamestown.org/ single/?no_cache=1&tx_ltnews[tt_news]=35006*.

64. *Ibid.*

65. *Ibid.*

66. Randy Boswell, "Russian reports suggest conflict over Arctic possible," Canwest News Service, May 13, 2009.

67. Available from *www.timesonline.co.uk/tol/news/world/article6859007.ece*.

68. Russian News and Information Agency Novosti, "Four Russian Strategic Bombers Patrol Arctic, Atlantic Oceans," June 20, 2008, available from *en.rian.ru/russia/20080620/111462629.html*; "Russian Navy Planes Patrol the Arctic," June 11, 2008, available from *en.rian.ru/russia/20080611/110061305.html*; "Russian Tu-160 Bombers Continue Patrols over the Arctic," *RIA Novosti*, June 11, 2008, available from *en.rian.ru/russia/20080611/110039789.html*; Interfax, "Russian Strategic Bombers Tracked by NATO Jets While on Mission over Arctic," June 10, 2008.

69. Interfax, "Russian Strategic Bombers Patrolling Arctic," June 9, 2008.

70. Rowan Scarborough, "Russian Flights Smack of Cold War," *The Washington Times*, June 26, 2008, pp. A1, A17.

71. Russian News and Information Agency Novosti, "Russian Bombers Conduct Patrols Along South American Coast," September 16, 2008, available from *en.rian.ru/russia/20080916/116834364. html*; ITAR-TASS, "Four Russian Missile Carriers Patrolling Arctic, Atlantic Oceans," July 9, 2008, and "Russian Strategic Bombers Continue Arctic, Atlantic Patrols," Russian News and Information Agency Novosti, July 9, 2008, available from *en.rian.ru/russia/20080709/113588157.html*.

72. Russian News and Information Agency Novosti, "Russian Navy to Expand Presence in Arctic, Atlantic, Pacific," June 10, 2008, available from *en.rian.ru/russia/20080610/109836278.html*; Interfax, "Russian Navy to Increase Presence in Atlantic, Pacific, Northern Latitudes—Defense Ministry," June 10, 2008; Russian News and Information Agency Novosti, "Russia Prepares for Future Combat in the Arctic," June 24, 2008, available from *en.rian. ru/russia/20080624/111915879.html*.

73. Russian News and Information Agency Novosti, "Russian Navy to Expand Presence in Arctic, Atlantic, Pacific."

74. Russian News and Information Agency Novosti, "Russian Navy Resumes Military Presence Near Spitsbergen," July 14, 2008, available from *en.rian.ru/world/20080714/113914174. html*; ITAR-TASS, "Russia Warships Resume Presence in Arctic Areas," July 14, 2008; Russian News and Information Agency Novosti, "Russian Warship Arrives in Norway for Northern Eagle 2008 Exercise," July 17, 2008, available from *en.rian.ru/russia/20080717/114226210.html*.

75. *Ibid.*

76. ITAR-TASS, "Govt to Find One bln rbls to Substantiate Arctic Shelf Claim," April 18, 2008, and Convention on the Continental Shelf, 1958.

77. Galeotti, "Cold Calling," p. 12; Doughton, "Aging Fleet Slows U.S. in Arctic 'Chess Game.'" Other source reports that

Russia has 20 icebreakers. See McCullough, "Coast Guard Gets $30M to Overhaul Icebreaker."

78. "Russia to Build New Icebreakers," *Barents Observer*, October 17, 2008, available from *barentsobserver.com/russia-to-build-new-icebreakers.4519572.html*; Russian News and Information Agency Novosti, "Russia Tests Nuclear Icebreaker on Open Sea," Space War, February 7, 2007, available from *www.spacewar.com/reports/Russia_Tests_Nuclear_Icebreaker_On_Open_Sea_999.html*; Nils Bøhmer *et al.*, *The Arctic Nuclear Challenge*, Oslo, Norway: Bellona Foundation, 2001, p. 39, available from *bellona.org/filearchive/fil_The_Arctic_Nuclear_Challenge.pdf*.

79. Russian News and Information Agency Novosti, "Russia Tests Nuclear Icebreaker on Open Sea," and "New Russian Nuclear Icebreaker 'Will Be Built by 2015,'" June 9, 2008, available from *en.rian.ru/russia/20080609/109670225.html*.

80. Russian News and Information Agency Novosti, "Medvedev Signs Law to Allot Off-Shore Deposits Without Auctions," August 18, 2008, available from *en.rian.ru/russia/20080718/114359207.html*.

81. Available from *arctic.foreignpolicyblogs.com/2009/09/25/russia-seeks-foreign-investors-for-arctic-gas-development/*.

82. "First sea drilling platform for Arctic begins testing," October 28, 2009, available from *www.zeenews.com/news574070.html*.

83. Agence France-Presse, "Russia's Putin Tours New Rig in Arctic Oil Drive," *Breitbart.com*, July 11, 2008, available from *www.breitbart.com/article.php?id=080711175151.j2k3z1z7*.

84. Available from *www.world-nuclear-news.org/NN-Russia_relocates_construction_of_floating_power_plant-1108084.html* .

85. "Russia to build floating Arctic nuclear stations."

86. Available from *www.world-nuclear-news.org/NN-Reactors_ready_for_first_floating_plant-0708094.html*.

87. Russia to build floating Arctic nuclear stations."

88. Available from *www.world-nuclear-news.org/NN-Russia_re-locates_construction_of_floating_power_plant-1108084.html* .

89. Thor Edward Jakobsson, "Climate Change and the Northern Sea Route: An Icelandic Perspective," Myron H. Nordquist, John Norton Moore, and Alexander S. Skaridov, eds., *International Energy, Policy, the Arctic and the Law of the Sea*, Leiden: The Netherlands, Martinus Nijhoff Publishers, 2005, pp. 292–293.

90. Maxim Krans, "Russia's Northern Sea Route: Just a Dotted Line on the Map?" *RIA Novosti*, May 23, 2007, available from *en.rian.ru/analysis/20070523/65989859.html*.

91. *Ibid.*

92. Marcell de Haas, "Russia's Arctic Strategy — challenge to Western energy security," Expert article 373, Baltic Rim Economies, August 31, 2009.

93. *Ibid.*

94. Roger McDermott, "Russia Planning Arctic Military Grouping," *Eurasia Daily Monitor*, Vol. 6, Issue 72, April 15, 2009.

95. *Ibid.*

96. "Fundamentals of Public Policy of the Russian Federation in the Arctic for the period up to 2020 and Beyond," September 18, 2008, available from *www.scrf.gov.ru/documents/98.html*.

97. *Ibid.*

98. Available from *arctic.foreignpolicyblogs.com/2009/11/01/russia-will-charge-ships-crossing-northern-sea-route/*.

99. *Ibid.*

100. Available from *georgewbush-whitehouse.archives.gov/news/releases/2009/01/20090112-3.html*.

101. Franklyn Griffiths, "New Illusions of a Northwest Passage," Myron H. Nordquist, John Norton Moore, and Alexander S. Skaridov, eds., *International Energy, Policy, the Arctic and the Law of the Sea*, Leiden, The Netherlands: Martinus Nijhoff Publishers, 2005, p. 304.

102. *Ibid.*

103. Associated Press, "Canada to Claim Arctic Passage," *The Washington Times*, August 20, 2007, available from *www.washingtontimes.com/news/2007/aug/20/canada-to-claim-arctic-passage*; and Eric Posner, "The New Race for the Arctic," *The Wall Street Journal*, August 3, 2007, available from *online.wsj.com/article/SB118610915886687045.html*.

104. Available from *arctic.foreignpolicyblogs.com/2009/12/03/the-canadian-northwest-passage/*.

105. "Canadian and US Arctic Gas Resources to Improve Energy Security," *Alexander's Gas & Oil Connections*, June 3, 2008, available from *www.gasandoil.com/goc/news/ntn82388.htm*.

106. National Research Council, *Polar Icebreakers*, p. 23.

107. North American Aerospace Defense Command, "About NORAD," Washington, DC: U.S. Department of Defense, available from *www.norad.mil/about/ANR.html*.

108. National Research Council, *Polar Icebreakers*, p. 50.

CHAPTER 2

THE ARCTIC:
A CLASH OF INTERESTS OR CLASH
OF AMBITIONS

Alexandr' Golts

Any observer who followed the statements of politicians as well as press coverage during the last 2 or 3 years must come to a definite conclusion: confrontation is growing in the Arctic region. Russia, which is planning to lodge a bid for the area, measuring 1.2 million square kilometers (km) with the United Nations Convention on the Law of the Sea, is ready to play a key role in the confrontation. Moscow has made several symbolically provocative gestures. In 2007, Artur Chilingarov, a famous Polar explorer and vice-speaker of the State Duma, led two Russian mini-submarines on a mission to stake Russia's claim to the region. The two submarines descended 2.5 miles (4 km) to the Arctic seabed, where they collected geological and water samples and dropped a titanium canister containing the Russian flag to bolster Russia's argument that the Lomonosov Ridge is an extension of its territory.

General Vladimir Shamanov, at that time Chief of Ministry of Defense (MOD) Main Directorate of Combat Training, stated in 2008 that "after the reaction of a certain number of heads of state to Russia's territorial claims to the continental plateau of the Arctic, the training division has immediately set out [training] plans for troops that could be engaged in Arctic combat missions." Shamanov mentioned that MOD made corrections in training plans for Leningrad, Siberian, and Far Eastern military districts so they would be ready to conduct operations in the region.[1]

A few months later, Shamanov, who in the meantime was appointed the Commander in chief of Russian Airborne Troops, announced that a team of Russian paratroopers was preparing for a symbolic landing at the Northern Pole to mark the 60th anniversary of a Cold War achievement by two Soviet scientists, who had landed at the North Pole in 1949. The proposed parachute drop was described by a top Russian general as a mission symbolizing the protection of national interests in the northern direction. Insisting that the operation would not stoke military tensions in the Arctic, General Vladimir Shamanov is quoted as saying: "We do not intend to engage in [saber-] rattling, we only intend to make a peaceful visit to the North Pole."[2]

In recent years, the Russian armed forces undertook several actions to demonstrate ambitions to control the Arctic region. In February 2009, Canadian fighter jets scrambled to intercept an approaching Russian bomber less than 24 hours before U.S. President Barack Obama's visit to Ottawa, Canada. In August 2009, two Russian attack submarines of Project 971 *Schuka-B* were sent to patrol Arctic regions near Canadian national borders. In the spring of 2009, Vice Admiral Oleg Burtsev, deputy head of the Navy Staff, said that Northern Fleet submarines will help in the protection and study of the Arctic shelf adjacent to the territory of Russia.[3]

North Atlantic Treaty Organization (NATO) spokesman James Appathurai's statement that the Arctic region is of high strategic importance to NATO in terms of providing security for allies received a tough reaction from the Russian side. "NATO lacked the technical capability to enhance its military presence in the Arctic. Only our country has the unique technical equipment capable of solving the problems of extreme Arctic conditions, and nothing can be compared with our fleet of icebreakers in terms of mobility and effectiveness," Artur Chilingarov said.[4]

"Plans for training the Navy of Russia will take into account the presence of NATO ships in the Arctic," said a senior representative of the Main Staff of the Navy of Russia to a RIA Novosti correspondent. He noted that Russia's military leadership will pay special attention to protecting national interests in the Arctic. "The main role here is assigned to nuclear submarines, which are the core of naval strategic nuclear forces of the country," said the source. He promised that the Navy is and will be ready to control marine areas "throughout the length of the northern sea borders of Russia." Chief of General Staff General Nikolai Makarov said that Russia should adequately respond to attempts to militarize the Arctic. "We watch what will be the degree of militarization of the region. Depending on this we will undertake adequate measures."[5] On April 18, 2008, at a meeting of the Maritime Collegium of the Russian government, Navy Commander Admiral Vladimir Vysotsky said that now there is peace and stability in the Arctic, but he did not exclude the possibility of territorial redistribution with the help of "armed intervention."[6]

These symbolic acts and militant statements were supported by doctrinal documents signed by Russian president Dmitry Medvedev. The most sensational part of the National Security Strategy adopted in May 2009 includes plans to create army units in Russia's Arctic region to "guarantee military security in different military-political situations." The strategy, approved by President Medvedev, declares the Arctic to be Russia's most important arena for international and military security in its relations with other countries. A coast guard unit of the Federal Security Service (FSB), the successor to the KGB, is planned to advance Russia's policy in the region. The strategy calls for the creation of an intelligence network to provide "effective control of economic, military, [and] ecological activity" in the Arctic.[7]

A few months earlier, in September 2008, the Security Council adopted "The fundamentals of Russian state policy in the Arctic up to 2020 and beyond," which outlines the country's strategy in the region, including the deployment of military, border, and coastal guard units "to guarantee Russia's military security in diverse military and political circumstances."[8] According to some sources, the Arctic Group of Forces will be part of the FSB, whose former chief and current secretary of the Security Council, Nikolai Patrushev, is a strong proponent of an aggressive state policy in the Arctic.

A few days before the adoption of the document on September 12, 2008, the Security Council of Russia held a meeting on strategic planning for "the problems of increasing the presence of Russia in the Arctic." Under the leadership of then-director of the FSB Nikolai Patrushev, the leading members of the Security Council (speakers of State Duma and Council Federation, defense and interior ministers, the heads of the FSB and SVR) went to Franz Josef Land where the outpost of the FSB Border Guards *Nagurskaya* is stationed, to discuss the buildup of a military presence. The meeting was presented as a symbolic act. "For the first time in the history of Russia's Security Council, the event of such a high rank is held outside the Arctic Circle," according to the official press release.[9]

All this creates the impression that Russia is seriously preparing to fight (including the use of military force) for possession of a huge Arctic space. Moscow filed a claim with the United Nations (UN) Commission on the Limits of the Continental Shelf (CLCS) in December 2001 with the hope of getting the rights to areas lying beyond its 200-mile zone. The matter at stake involves a territory exceeding 1.2 million square kilometers (km) in the Barents Sea, the Sea of Okhotsk, the Bering Strait, and the ice-free waters of the Arctic Ocean, which Russia views as its sovereign possessions. This claim rests on "Russian research of the earth's crust structure at the Mendeleyev Elevation in the Arctic Ocean that has proven the continental nature of many sections of the oceanic floor, which were previously attributed to the sub-oceanic type."[10]

Formally, Russia's claim does not contradict the norms of international maritime law. The Convention on the Law of the Sea passed by the UN in 1982 does envision an opportunity for littoral countries to expand their sovereign rights beyond the 200-mile exclusive economic zone — not infinitely, though, but only over those sections of the seabed of which the continental origins have been proved conclusively. Russia was the first country ever to lodge a claim with the CLCS; there is no mechanism for passing decisions of this kind. The UN regulations suggest that if a country lodging a claim agrees with the commission's recommendations, the latter are made public, after which the revised borders become final and mandatory.

The first attempt did not bring the desired result, as the CLCS asked for more convincing geological and geophysical evidence that the Mendeleyev and Lomonosov submerged ridges are extensions of Russia's continental shelf. Russia's intensive Arctic research carried out in 2005-07 and the symbolic culmination of this activity — the installation of the Russian tricolor on the sea floor — were called upon to add more weight to the official claim. The second claim will be filed not earlier then 2013.[11]

If successful, this theoretically would provide Moscow unbelievable wealth. It would have at its disposal the Northern Sea Route, which, together with the Northwest Passage, would give Russia the opportunity to control the shortest route between North America, Europe, and Asia. Moreover, if Moscow can prove its right to own a significant part of the Arctic Ocean, it will be allowed to develop oil and gas deposits. Experts estimate oil and gas deposits in the Russian part of the Arctic at 25 percent of the world's hydrocarbon reserves (approximately 15.5 billion tons of oil and 84.5 trillion cubic meters of gas). At present, Russia is already extracting up to 90 percent of the nickel and cobalt in the Arctic, 60 percent of the copper, 96 percent of platinoids, and 100 percent of apatite concentrate.[12]

Setting that aside, one should answer first of all the question of whether in the foreseeable future there is any realistic opportunity to obtain the wealth of the Arctic. All hopes are connected with the theory of melting Arctic ice. But this is only theory, not a *fait accompli*, as some authors insist.[13] The basis for predictions is the fact that from 1980 to 2007 mankind witnessed the melting of Arctic ice by 14 percent. At the same time, representatives of different schools of thought contend that the melting is no more than a change in the cyclic fluctuations of climate over the past 400 years, and an attempt to make predictions based on data of the past 30 years is simply incorrect.[14] Such skepticism is validated by the fact that during the last 2 years the process of melting ice stopped and began to grow.

However, even those who believe in the prospects for the release of the Arctic Ocean from ice, such as the former Prime Minister of Norway, believe that it would not occur until 2040. "The Arctic area would be of interest in 50 or 100 years — not now," said Lars Kullerud, President of the University of the Arctic.[15]

Previous forecasts had predicted the Arctic would be ice-free in summers towards the end of the 21st century. The most rationally-minded representatives of Russian official circles, for example, *charge d'affaires* of Russia in Canada, Sergei Petrov, have expressed their skepticism. He publically insisted that very few people take into account how difficult it would be to extract the resources buried beneath the ice and permafrost. He said that even the generation of his children probably will not see how to get resources from the deeper parts of the ocean floor. In the meantime, the dispute revolves around the very few sites suitable for development today, he said.[16] In addition, there is absolutely no guarantee that in 50 years, oil and gas will play the same important role in the global economy as they do now.

The revival of the Northern Sea Route was one of the ideas that preoccupied Russian President Vladimir Putin for all of the past decade. A campaign advertising the would-be glamorous prospects for Arctic navigation was one of the first electoral ploys when he was acting president. In April 2000, addressing a special conference on the Northern Sea Route and Russian shipbuilding convened on board the *Arktika* nuclear icebreaker in Murmansk, Putin gave assurances that the volume of cargo shipments in the Arctic might reach more than 10 million tons a year in the not-so-distant future, while the actual volume barely exceeded a million tons at the time.

Putin named several factors calling attention to the Northern Sea Route. He said that Russia needed "a state navigation policy, and the Arctic transport system offers a perfect testing range for that." He also stated that "the North has the riches that may soon be needed not only by Russia, but by all of humankind as well." That is why "Northern territories are our strategic reserve for the future." This led him to the logical conclusion that "the Northern Sea Route is an important factor for ensuring the state's security."[17]

In reality, the Northern Sea Route still remains Russia's internal navigation passage that is used, at the very most, for transporting short-haul export resources, metal ores, and hydrocarbons. Hopes for using this route for transit cargo shipments between Europe and Asia were short-lived, and the discussions of the prospects for the Northern Sea Route have been down-played of late even in Russia itself. Vyacheslav Ruksha, general director of "Atomflot" and ex-director of the Federal Marine and River Transport Agency, admitted in public that cargo shipments along the Northern Sea Route cannot be profitable at the moment because this passage includes sections like the Sannikov Strait and Vilkitsky Strait, which are a mere 17 meters or so deep. This limits the tonnage of cargo ships, making the southern route between Europe and Asia, although it is longer, much less expensive due to the greater tonnage of transiting ships. "Transport activity on the Northern Sea Route is a sensitive indicator of the economy of the state," Vyacheslav Ruksha insists. "In the Soviet years, we transported 7 million tons of cargo, by the end of the century, only 1.4 million. Now freight traffic has exceeded 2 million and continues to grow."[18] Until now, passage of goods along the Northern Sea Route has been unprofitable!

Such became clear even from the triumphant report to Putin by Sergei Frank, head of Sovkomflot, Russia's largest ocean carrier. According Frank, the through-traffic Northern Sea Route would not be started in full until the summer of 2010. At that time, Russia was expected to exercise only some "pilot runs," which he referred to as "innovation challenges." Furthermore, it was quite possible, he said, that "we will sail north of the New Siberian Islands, as there are certain restrictions on planting in the Laptev Strait and the Sannikov Strait."[19]

But that requires other ships. Ruksha said that fair prospects still existed in shipping in the Central Arctic rather than along the Northern Sea Route. This has a hitch, too, as completely new powerful transport ships and icebreakers will be needed, as "the ice there is completely different."[20]

As for the new ships, the situation is bleak. It is true that Russia has the biggest icebreaker fleet. The problem is that the Russian fleet has seven rapidly-aging nuclear icebreakers that facilitate navigation along the Northern Sea Route. Even considering all the imaginable extensions of service life, the *Arktika* has practically exhausted its service life; the *Rossiya* is also in its death throes; the *Taimyr* may last until 2013; the *Vaigach* and the *Sovietsky Soyuz* until 2014; and the *Yamal* until 2017. The *Fifty Years of Victory* icebreaker that the Murmansk shipping line commissioned in 2007 can just barely be considered a new one, since its construction at the Baltic Shipyards in St. Petersburg, Russia, dragged on for almost 20 years. This means that it, too, belongs to the old family of icebreakers. The only achievement is the recent launch of the tanker *Kirill Lavrov*, which is said to be capable of breaking ice up to 1 to 2 meters thick. An unpleasant fact was mentioned very frankly by such a "pro-imperialist" figure as Deputy Prime Minister Sergei Ivanov:

> Only one company is engaged in ice shipbuilding, [and] there are very few icebreaking ships that were launched. As he did 10 years ago, Vladimir Putin still demands that the management of the shipbuilding industry develop a multiyear program.
>
> But even if there is an opportunity for access to lucrative transit routes and to the deposits of natural resources, the question remains whether Russia has the tools to use them. Assuming that the ice will disappear (there are still no oil production technologies on the drifting ice), Russia does not have the technology for deep water oil production. Lately in the Arctic seas not even a single parametric well was drilled.[21]

Unfortunately, the absence of rational reasons for the confrontation over Arctic access does not always exclude the possibility of confrontation. At present, Russia is showing (at least in words) the intention to strengthen its military capabilities in the Arctic region. Does Russia have any opportunities to do so?

First of all, one should keep in mind that the military dimension always played a key role in the development of the Arctic region. Beginning at least in the 1930s, the Soviet and then Russian military have been the overlords of the Arctic, although the role that was attached to the region in the country's strategic security would fluctuate depending on the foreign policy context. The Soviet authorities looked at the Arctic from different angles. During World War II, communication lines linking the Soviet Union with its allies in the anti-Nazi coalition were laid in the Arctic region. After the Cold War began, the Arctic became the front line in an imaginary nuclear war with the United States, as it was in the Arctic that Soviet strategists expected the approach of strategic bombers or ballistic missiles from across the North Pole. Testing grounds (Novaya Zemlya, Plesetsk, and Nenoksa) where the Soviet Union, as a nuclear superpower, tested its armaments were also located in deserted Arctic regions.

The *Basics of State Policy of the Russian Federation in the Arctic Region*, Russia's main national Arctic doctrinal document, which the Russian government endorsed in 2001, concentrated on military issues much more than did the 2008 document. It insisted that "all types of activity in the Arctic are tied to the interests of defense and security to the maximum degree." The list of priorities features as Item #1 the "reliable functioning of the Russian Navy's group of strategic sea-based nuclear forces deployed there for deterring the threats of aggression against the Russian Federation and its allies." Item #2 is "reliable control over the state border of the Russian Federation and Arctic maritime areas in order to defend the Russian Federation's national interests in the region."[22]

Ironically, in the 1990s, which was a period of total decay of Russian armed forces, the Arctic region had a military role. The ensuing shrinkage of national nuclear arsenals has led to a situation in which sea-based nuclear forces became Russia's main instrument of deterrence over the short term. While Soviet-era Moscow put the main emphasis on land-based intercontinental ballistic missiles (ICBMs), in the 1990s submarines formed the backbone of Russian security. Furthermore, the aim of making Russian submarines invulnerable rested on the concept of the so-called "Strategic Northern Bastion."

This concept flowered in the Russian Defense Ministry in 1992. Its authors believed that a sharp drop in Russia's defense capability simultaneously in all theaters of naval operations and scarce finances allocated for defense programs made it necessary to concentrate the main group of nuclear forces in the Northern Fleet, which operates in the Arctic. It suggested the concealment of submarine missile cruisers from an adversary under the meters-thick Arctic ice, as Russian nuclear submarines would become the enemy's natural targets in case of an armed conflict. The Arctic looked like an ideal region for erecting this bastion for another reason: Russia had obvious advantages over other countries in that it had many years of experience in scientific research in sub-polar waters.

Attempts to create the Strategic Northern Bastion enjoyed such a priority that even during the economic crisis of the 1990s, the Northern Fleet received some funding. As a result, in the most difficult period for the Russian armed forces, the Northern Fleet obtained the nuclear cruiser *Peter the Great*. Today, the Northern Fleet is the most effective component of Russia's Navy (two-thirds of Russian naval power is concentrated in the Northern Fleet). All the bases of the Northern Fleet are located in the Arctic region: Severomorsk, Polaryarnoye, Gadzhievo, Ostrovnoye, Nerpichya Guba, Olenya Guba, Sayda-Guba, Bolshaya Lopatka, Iokange (Gremikha), Granite, and Vidyaevo. A marine infantry brigade is located in Sputnik and Pechenga.

Forces of the Northern Fleet are comprised of 11 strategic submarines, 3 nuclear submarines with cruise missiles, 6 nuclear torpedo submarines, 38 I rank ships, 20 II rank ships, 19 III rank ships, 130 boats, and the marine infantry brigade with 74 tanks and 209 artillery systems. Northern Fleet aviation had 20 Tu-22Ms (bombers), 12 Su-25s (FGA), 24 Su-27s (FTR), 2 An-12s, 25 An-12s/An-24s/An-26s (TPT), and 27 Ka-27s/Ka-29s (ASW helicopters).[23] Apart from the Northern Fleet Russian sector, the Arctic is a zone of responsibility divided among the four military districts: the Leningrad Military District, from Pechengi (Murmansk region) to Ust-Kora (Arkhangelsk region); the Volga-Urals Military District, from Yar to the island Olenyi (Yamalo-Nenets Autonomous District); the Zone of the Siberian Military District, from Leskinen to Kozhevnikovo (Krasnoyarskyi Krai); and the Far East Military District, from the island of Bolshoi Begichev (Republic of Sakha Yakutia) to Anadyr (Chukotkyi Autonomous District).

Most of the Russian armed forces and resources in the Arctic region are located mainly in the Murmansk region (two motorized rifle brigades). The Central Test Ground (Novaya Zemlya), where nuclear weapons were tested, and the main center for missile testing (Plesetsk) are in the Arkhangelsk region. Monitoring stations of the Space Forces are on the Novaya Zemlya and in Plesetsk and Naryan-Mar. Long-Range Aviation forces use airfields in Rogachevo (Novaya Zemlya) and Vorkuta.[24]

Some support units of the Strategic Missile Forces are located in the northern zone of the Volga-Urals Military District (Nenets Autonomous District). A station for monitoring ICBM trajectories is located in Noril'sk (the northern zone of the Siberian Military District troops). An airfield for long-range aviation is also located in Norilsk.[25] Stations for ICBM launches monitoring are located in Yakutsk and Mirny (Far Eastern Military District). The 72th Fighter Regiment is also located in Amderma (Anadyr) in the Far Eastern Military District and an anti-electronic warfare

(AEW) regiment is in Pechora Kamenka. Airfields for Long-Range Aviation are located in Chekurovka, Tiksi-3, and Anadyr.[26]

It is important to mention that all the foregoing data relate to the period before 2009. One can suppose that now, when the number of units of ground forces has been reduced by a factor of 11, and Navy and Air Force units by a factor of two, number of Russian troops in the Arctic has also been reduced. The information is rather contradictory. On one hand, newspapers insist that Russia at least partially restored the garrisons in the places where they were previously stationed such as Franz Josef Land and Novaya Zemlya, but in reduced numbers.[27] On the other hand, it was mentioned at the hearings in the Federation Council that "airfields for long-range strategic bombers at Anadyr, Vorkuta, and Tiksi will be closed in the near future as part of military reform."[28]

Some idea of Russia's current military presence is given in official information by the MOD on the amount of supplies for the winter northern garrisons.[29] But does presence mean that Russia will be able to back their claims with military force? In fact, the entire military presence (most of it is Navy) is concentrated only on the Kola Peninsula; all the rest of the huge space up to the Chukotka strip has no combat units. The construction of the modern border complex "Nagurski" on the archipelago, Zemlya Franza Josefa (Franz Josef Island) should be followed by the creation of similar complexes on Wrangel Island and then all across the Arctic coast. The first time in many years that border patrol ships traversed the Northern Sea Route in the Chukotskoye Sea was in 2008.

The United States can use the ships of the Atlantic Fleet as well as the Pacific Fleet in the Arctic region.

It has 30-40 combat ships, including aircraft carriers, attack submarines, and destroyers. The Norwegian, Danish, and Canadian navies together have four destroyers, 30 frigates, and 11 submarines. Their navies are trained to conduct warfare in the Arctic region.

NATO forces can rely on a powerful system of bases, while the Russian Northern Fleet can base only on the Kola Peninsula. The superiority of NATO in the air, too, is clear: the carriers it has transport 400 combat aircraft. The *Admiral Kuznetsov* carrier has on board only 12 aircraft. There also is a land-based Tu-22M3 regiment, an anti-submarine squadron, and an anti-submarine helicopter regiment. Ground forces operating east of the Barents Sea and Novaya Zemlya in fact have no bases nor prospect of ground and air support. Russian forces are thus insufficient if authorities are seriously thinking in terms of a possible military confrontation. It has become obvious that Russian military potential in the Arctic is much lower than the united potential of the NATO countries. Experts insist that Russia has to establish an additional fleet which can control its northern coast from the Urals to west of Chukotka. Possible areas of responsibility of such a fleet are the eastern part of the Kara Sea, Laptev Sea, and the eastern part of the East Siberian Sea, with locations in Dixon, Khatanga, and Tiksi.

Fortunately, there is no sign of the development of such a fleet. It is no coincidence that soon after the announcement of the intention to "create a force for the Arctic," Moscow pretty soon back-pedaled. Foreign Minister Sergei Lavrov declared:

> We do not intend to increase our armed presence in
> the Arctic. Decisions being adopted to strengthen the
> capabilities of the coast guard are important for rescue

operations in these areas. There are no plans to intro-
duce any extra armed forces in addition to the regular
units performing their functions.[30]

Obviously, the creation of Arctic troop comple-
ments does not advance the new image of the armed
forces (as Russian leadership prefers to describe a
radical military reform). It is a clear example of the
contradiction between the realistic plans for a military
buildup, which orients the conventional armed forces
toward local conflicts, and the militaristic rhetoric of
the Kremlin underlining the willingness of Russian
armed forces to participate in a confrontation with
NATO countries.

But even if Russia has managed not only to restore
the combat potential of the Soviet armed forces, but
even to raise it dramatically, that fact can hardly help
advance Russia's territorial claims. All Soviet and then
Russian military infrastructure has been established
to provide nuclear deterrence. However, the ability to
launch a nuclear strike against the United States adds
little to the ability to defend the interests of Russia
in the Arctic. That is a fundamentally different military task. Ironically, these two tasks contradict each
other.[31] Moreover, I suspect that any Russian attempt
to use military force to achieve its stated goals in the
Arctic has no rational explanation. In that region, the
interests and claims of the United States, Canada,
Denmark, Norway, and Russia are in mutual conflict.
For example, the United States has territorial disputes
with Canada, Russia has disputes with Norway. With
each country focused on its own interests, Moscow
has much room to maneuver for it may enter into alliances with one against the other, to compromise, or
pursue its own goals. However, this diplomatic game

is possible only as long as Russia desists from threatening its opponents with military force. But as soon as it dares to use military threats, arrangements of collective defense of NATO countries will inevitably be activated. Instead of bargaining and making tactical alliances with individual countries, Russia will be forced to confront a united front of Western countries.

Thus, on the one hand, the wealth of the Arctic appears to be at least questionable. On the other hand, military force cannot bolster Russia's claim. A cold war in the Arctic is unthinkable. We therefore ask why Moscow has pursued a confrontational approach with such persistence, attracting worldwide opprobrium in the process. One reason is that other Arctic nations have signaled their willingness to use force. The United States and Canada regularly conduct military exercises in the Arctic region. Denmark has planned to develop special Arctic military units. All sides have exaggerated their readiness for military confrontation.

In my opinion, today the Arctic is an ideal field for the expression of great power ambitions. It allows politicians to grab the headlines and demonstrate their patriotism to voters. The Arctic is a region where the interests of Moscow and Washington, former global adversaries, clash at least theoretically. Thus, the Arctic is a great stage on which to play a parody of the cold war. Indeed, the entire foreign policy of Russia is now a parody of its foreign policy during the Cold War era. It is the international policy of Vladimir Putin. In his famous "Munich" speech, Putin as much as suggested to the West that Russia would play the role of the Soviet Union and even the Warsaw Pact. Putin insisted that the basis of its relationship with the West still lay in the military balance. This confrontation should remain solely rhetorical (in the last 10 years, there has been no real step that could be interpreted as a threat to the West). But such a pose as Putin's requires the creation of situations in which maintaining a military balance would make some sort of sense. At the present time, such sense applies primarily in the sphere of strategic weapons. However, due to the rejection by the Obama administration of U.S. deployment of strategic missile defense elements in Poland and the Czech Republic, as well as U.S. agreement to concluding a new treaty on strategic offensive armaments, the number of opportunities to simulate a military confrontation greatly narrowed. In this situation, the Arctic appears to be an ideal field in which to rattle the militaristic saber.

ENDNOTES - CHAPTER 2

1. Available from *www.redstar.ru/2008/06/24_06/1_02.html*.

2. Available from *www.kommersant.ru/doc.aspx?DocsID=121 8499*.

3. Available from *www.rian.ru/defense_safety/20090323/16574 4281.html*.

4. Available from *www.rian.ru/world/20090212/161897296.html*.

5. Available from *news.mail.ru/politics/2391311/*.

6. Vladimir Voronov, *Severnii Front*, available from *Profil 112(615) 06.04.2009*.

7. Available from *www.scrf.gov.ru/documents/99.html*.

8. Available from *www.scrf.gov.ru/documents/98.html*.

9. Available from *www.profile.ru/numbers/?number=653*.

10. *Ibid.*

11. Aleksandr Gasyuk, *"Spori ushli na dno,"* *Rossiiskaya gazeta,* June 23, 2009.

12. Available from *www.globalaffairs.ru/numbers/39/12359.html.*

13. Scott G. Borgerson, "Arctic Meltdown: The Economic and Security Implications of Global Warming," *Foreign Affairs,* March/April 2008.

14. Ian Eisenman, Norbert Untersteiner, and J. S. Wettlaufer, "On the reliability of simulated Arctic sea ice in Global Climate Models," *Geophysical Research Letters* 34: L10501, 2007, available from *doi:10.1029/2007GL029914.*

15. "Arctic nations say no Cold War; military stirs," *Reuters,* June 21, 2009,

16. Available from *www.inosmi.ru/translation/250320.html.*

17. Available from *www.globalaffairs.ru/numbers/32/9779.html.*

18. Sergei Leskov, "Led.Moros Russkii reactor," *Isvestia,* December 1, 2009.

19. Available from *www.advis.ru/cgi-bin/new.pl?7F9B7D9E-DE49-DC41-B802-7183D7DED974.*

20. Leskov.

21. Available from *www.rg.ru/2009/06/22/ivanov.html.*

22. Available from *eng.globalaffairs.ru/numbers/24/1218.html.*

23. Voenno-politicheskie stranitsi, Ves rossiyiskii flot. Vlast.№7 (760) от 25.02.2008; Konstantin Chuprin. Vooruzhennie sili stran SNG i Baltii, Minsk, 2009.

24. Vsya rossiiskaya armiya.Vlast.№7 (610) от 21.02.2005.

25. *Ibid.*

26. *Ibid.*

27. Nikolai Poroskov, Effect "Titanika," Vremya novostei 16.11.2009.

28. Available from *www.forum-mil.ru/news/2009-12-17-172.*

29. During the 2009 navigation period, 99.6 thousand tons of cargo were shipped to remote garrisons. Of these, dry goods (food and military-technical materiel), 44.2 thousand tons; liquid cargo (fuel and lubricants, fuel oil, diesel fuel, etc.) 55.4 thousand tons. In the far North (Northern Fleet), wintering stocks for the period of navigation were provided to 59 garrisons. In the Far East (Pacific Fleet), delivery was made to 126 points. In addition, wintering stocks were brought in for deployment of the units of the Leningrad Military District and the Far East Military District, available from *www.mil.ru/info/1069/details/index.shtml?id=69707.*

30. Available from *www.mid.ru/Brp_4.nsf/arh/CFA4407CF5842 0EAC32575A800255D59?OpenDocument.*

31. Inter-University Seminar on Armed Forces and Society, July 29, 2009, available from *afs.sagepub.com at.*

CHAPTER 3

RUSSIAN MILITARY PRESENCE IN THE HIGH NORTH:
PROJECTION OF POWER AND CAPACITIES OF ACTION

Marlène Laruelle

At a time when large scientific expeditions are scarce, the conquest of the Arctic brings back an air of romantic adventure to great power discourse, but also signals the return of nationalist rhetoric. The phenomenon is not unique to Russia. Ottawa, Canada, also seems to build the Arctic as a new Canadian flagship. The decision—approved almost unanimously by the House of Commons in spite of protests from northern Inuit communities—to change the name of the Northwest Passage to the "Canadian Northwest Passage" confirmed the state susceptibility in respect to territorial sovereignty in the Arctic.[1] In Russia, the conquest of the High North is an identity-building project.[2] The president's special representative for cooperation in the Arctic and Antarctic, famous polar explorer and member of United Russia, Arthur Chilingarov, does not hesitate to celebrate Russian ambitions in the Arctic. During the Polar Year 2007, leading the highly publicized Russian expedition to the North Pole, he planted a Russian flag on the seabed of the Arctic, asserting rights for those who arrive first,[3] while in 2009, he again said it bluntly that "we will not give the Arctic to anyone."[4]

Verbose rhetoric aside, taking into account the realities of climate extremes makes players much more modest and hesitant than they wish to admit. The dominance of the Arctic, in addition to questions of the environment and the rights of indigenous peoples, poses a real technological, human, and financial challenge. The economics of this venture have not yet been demonstrated and depend on long-term climatic changes that are difficult to measure and cannot really be assessed until the time frame 2020-30. For Moscow, however, the issue remains crucial: its future as an energy great power is an Arctic future. For the past few years, Russia has thus faced a revival of strategic thinking on the High North. Behind the nationalist-tinged discourse, which is fairly aggressive towards the West, Russia's goals are far more pragmatic: attempts to reform the army, upgrade the navy, modernize the Northern Fleet, increase civil-military cooperation, and resurrect the shipyard sector. The traditional Russian gaps between rhetoric and reality, and power projection and actual capabilities, are especially important since the Arctic is uncharted territory.

RUSSIA'S NEW STRATEGIC THINKING ABOUT THE ARCTIC

The High North occupies a very specific place in Russian defense strategy. Since the 1950s, this region has been host to key industries and infrastructure related to the Russian nuclear deterrent, particularly the installations on the Kola Peninsula, which have to be secured. The High North also guarantees access to the Atlantic Ocean and is therefore vital to the Russian Navy, which it needs for its international missions, especially since Russia lost several ports in the Baltic Sea and the Black Sea (Paldiski in Estonia and the question of Sevastopol in the Ukraine) following the breakup of the Soviet Union. The High North borders Norwegian and Danish zones under North Atlantic Treaty Organization (NATO) control in which the North Alliance conducts simulation exercises that the Kremlin interprets as "aggressive." Lastly, the High North has a symbolic significance concerning Russia's status as a great power. The Stalinist myth of the Northern Maritime Route, *Sevmorput'*, used in the 1930s and 1940s to exert Russia's military and industrial prowess, is reemerging today.[5] Above all, energy interests linked to the exploitation of sub-sea and continental shelf resources have profoundly revived the region's strategic importance.[6]

The revival of strategic interest in the High North materialized in the early 2000s, with an initial strategy for the Arctic published in 2001 but hardly implemented, and then a report completed in 2004 by the Russian State Council Working Group on National Security Interests in the North. During his second term, Vladimir Putin increased his references to the important role of the region. Several texts were adopted: a new Russian maritime doctrine until 2020; a policy plan for naval construction; a development plan for naval transport in Russia; a development plan for the fishing industry; the foundations for Russian policy in the field of maritime military activities; and a defense strategy for state borders, inland waters, territorial seas, the continental shelf, and the exclusive economic zones of Russia. The Maritime College, meanwhile, is in charge of changing Russian strategic thinking. The new Russian maritime doctrine includes a naval fleet, merchant shipping, a fishing fleet, and research vessels, in a holistic approach to the exploitation of the sea. In September 2008, a new strategy for the Arctic through 2020 was adopted, and Dmitri Medvedev explicitly portrayed the Arctic as a base for Russian natural resources in the 21st century.[7] The National Security Strategy of the Russian Federation to 2020, released in May 2009, underlines the battle that is taking place for energy resources, considered to be the potential means for Russia to remain a great power. The document confirms Russia's interest in the Arctic, which is elevated to the status of the Caspian Sea and Central Asia, as one of the main energy battlegrounds of the future.

On the strategic level, in the summer of 2008, Russia changed course, confirming it was expanding its current level of operations in the Arctic. The Russian Navy announced that its fleet was resuming a warship presence in the Arctic, and ever since military ships have patrolled near Norwegian and Danish defense zones. The stakes are fundamental since the Russian fleet cannot enter the Atlantic except by passing through specific choke points, two being the junction of Greenland, Iceland, and Norway, and the junction of Greenland, Iceland, and the United Kingdom.[8] Moscow has paid particular attention to the situation in the Svalbard archipelago, which it interprets as indicative of global tensions between NATO and Russia. The Russian Army therefore wants to increase its protection of the Russian settlement at Barentsburg and provide more effective protection for Russian fishermen, who are often arrested by the Norwegian navy. In the summer of 2008, Russian military exercises were organized close to Spitzbergen involving the cruisers *Marshall Ustinov* and the *Severomorsk*, with the plan now being to hold these exercises at regular intervals. Director of National Fisheries (*Goskomrybolovstvo*) Andrei Krainin has asked the armed force to give "psychological support" to Russian fishermen navigating close to Norwegian waters.[9] The Russian

Navy is also increasing the operational radius of the Northern Fleet's submarines, and under-ice training for submariners is becoming a priority task. Naval activism in the Arctic is accompanied by a new dynamics in aviation. In 2008, strategic bombers flew over the Arctic for the first time since the end of the Cold War. Two Ty-95s, based in Saratov on the Engels aviation base with inflight refueling capability, now regularly patrol the Arctic.[10] These over-flights drew criticism from Canada, which has accused them of coming too close to Canadian territory. Two new aircraft squadrons are apparently going to be created to supervise naval operations in the Arctic.

Lieutenant General Vladimir Shamanov, director of the Central Directorate of Military Training and Troop Services (GUBD) at the Ministry of Defense, announced plans to establish an Arctic special forces unit (*spetsnaz*) to support Russia's northern policy. To justify his decision, he made reference to the North Region-2008 exercise undertaken by the United States in Alaska, which involved more than 5,000 military personnel.[11] The current administrative apportionment within the Defense Ministry is going to be reviewed so that specialized sections can be created to cover the High North. This process will involve regrouping of sections of the troops placed with the military districts of Leningrad, Siberia, and the Far East within a future Arctic district. These troops are going to have to be particularly mobile, will probably have an icebreaker assigned to their unit, and are due to be operational by 2016. Moreover, the Institute of the Armed Forces at Ryazan could be endowed with an "Arctic faculty" for training new specialists.[12] Provisions will likely also be made to strengthen FSB control over the region to deal with the new threats that have arisen because of the exploitation of the continental shelf and the proliferation of maritime traffic: border control systems, the introduction of special visa regulations to certain regions, and the implementation of technological controls over fluvial zones and sites along the northern maritime route.[13]

However, as General Shamanov is known for his provocative declarations, these statements are difficult to interpret because they took place within a framework of ideological escalation. The usual difficulties of the Russian army to put into practice these calls for change suggest that the birth of Arctic brigades will probably be a long and chaotic administrative process.

RUSSIA'S NEW NAVAL AMBITIONS

The strengthening of Russian military presence in the High North is closely linked to the new naval ambitions of Russia. The Russian Navy hopes to become the second most powerful in the world in 20 to 30 years. In 2008 and 2009, Moscow displayed its former Soviet traditions by organizing several long-range cruises, the most numerous since the fall of the Soviet Union, in different parts of the world, for example, sending the nuclear-powered guided missile cruiser *Peter the Great* to the Mediterranean and Caribbean seas, South Atlantic, and the Indian oceans. The modernization of the Russian Navy is based on the construction of a new fleet of nuclear submarines, the abandonment of single-function vessels in favor of multipurpose and more mobile ones, and the production of six squadrons of aircraft carriers, which would propel the Russian Navy to second in the world in terms of combat capability. However, this phase of construction will not begin until 2015 and will be extremely costly, making its implementation iffy and dependent on the global economic performance of the country.[14]

Moreover, these naval ambitions should be viewed in the context of the modernization troubles experienced by the Russian Army. The money that has been pumped into the military sector during Vladimir Putin's two terms—the army's budget increased 500 percent in 8 years—does not in itself constitute reform. On the contrary, there was a partial return to the pathologies of the Soviet Army.[15] The military elite has had difficulties in understanding the stakes of recruiting conscripts in a country in full demographic crisis and of accepting the idea of alternative service and professional recruitment. Hazing (*dedovshchina*) goes largely unpunished, corruption among officers is massive, professionalism and discipline are in decline, and the quality of military tactics in difficult terrain has not improved between Afghanistan and the two wars in Chechnya.

For more than 2 decades, Russian military doctrines have been rather vague about how to define the enemy, oscillating between the West in general and NATO in particular, on the one hand, and the small separatist movements and international terrorism on the other. Russia's definition of the enemy brings with it fundamental military decisions, particularly concerning the ability to change to a professional army, which would be smaller but better trained and equipped. The reform plan announced at the end of 2008 anticipates a large transformation of the Russian Army to fewer men who are more mobile, better educated, and better equipped. For this, the officer corps is set for a reduction on the order of 150,000-200,000 men by 2012.[16] Those separated will be transferred to the reserves. However, this modernization is coming along slower than expected, raising doubts from some parts of the Ministry of Defense.

Within the armed forces, the navy had been the biggest loser from the drastic reduction of military budgets in the 1990s. It saw its share of the defense budget drop from 23 percent to 9 percent. In addition, the objectives mentioned in the two state programs to modernize the armed forces (1996-2005 and 2001-10) were never achieved. The third State Program for the Armed Forces (2007-15) finally signaled the return of the navy and its symbolic and financial reassessment. For the first time in several decades, it has been placed on an equal footing with other services, and one-quarter of the budget is dedicated to building new ships. However, this number seems insufficient. It can support the construction of two or three new nuclear submarines, but those currently in service also have urgent repair needs.[17] Moreover, in 2008, the state allocated only 10 percent of the sum necessary for these repairs.[18]

Russian shipyards have long lacked public funding, are based on old technologies, and are too oriented toward the military, while civilian industry is in greater demand. To remedy this imbalance, the government has planned investments of more than 170 billion rubles ($5.5 billion) for the development of shipyards between 2010 and 2015, according to the official text on the main directions of state industrial policy and its realization in the field of shipbuilding. This is indeed one of the three priority areas the Kremlin has identified to revive domestic industry, along with aviation and space.

Modernization of the Russian Navy is a strategic imperative for the High North and the Pacific Fleet, and the Khabarovsk, Nikolaevsk on Amur, and Komsomolsk on Amur shipyards. All of the Russian fleets have a desperate need for coastal vessels, especially corvettes, the shortage of which endangers the safety of the Russian coast. The navy must also consider its needs for new aircraft carriers. As in Europe and the United States, technological needs have become more complex, and the trend is toward more versatile hardware. The revival of shipbuilding is very costly and demanding in terms of technology and know-how. Russia will likely suffer a lack of vessels, mainly coastal, for several years; old ones will be decommissioned, with new ones not yet out of the yards.

MODERNIZING THE NORTHERN FLEET AND THE NUCLEAR DETERRENT

The Northern Fleet, based close to Murmansk in the north of the Kola Peninsula at Severomorsk, remains the most powerful of the four Russian fleets (Pacific, Baltic, Black Sea, and Caspian). It contains the largest number of icebreakers and nuclear submarines; about two-thirds of the Russian Navy's nuclear force is based there. It is in charge of all operations in the Atlantic and is thus able to venture as far as the Caribbean or to conduct anti-pirate operations close to the Gulf of Aden.

The Northern Fleet was hit hard by the fall of the Soviet Union. In 1986, it comprised some 180 nuclear-powered submarines of different classes, while today it has been reduced by three-quarters to just 42. In addition, its history is marked by several failures. A total of four submarines have sunk, including the *Kursk* in 2000, and its ballistic missile launches regularly fail. The fleet also faces numerous problems related to its aging vessels, the naval nuclear fuel cycle, the disposal of radioactive waste, and contamination issues. The naval nuclear reactors concentrated in this region are dangerous, many of the nuclear submarines waiting to be decommissioned are poorly secured, and large amounts of nuclear waste remain stored on vessels specially designed for dumping at sea.[19] Approximately 25,000 spent fuel assemblies removed from submarines are located at Northern Fleet facilities, mostly at Andreyeva Bay and Gremikha, then shipped and loaded into rail containers for processing at Mayak. Since 2001, Atomflot has been overseeing a liquid radioactive waste processing facility. Even if tens of new containers are being financed by the Arctic Military Environmental Cooperation (AMEC) project,[20] the situation remains fragile on the environmental level and greatly concerns Russian's northern neighbors.

The Northern Fleet has close to 80 operational ships of different categories, while 30+ are being repaired or are on stand-by.[21] Their average age is 20 years. The fleet's nuclear-powered submarines consist of 11 ballistic missile submarines (SSBNs), four cruise missile submarines (SSGNs), and about 20 multipurpose attack submarines (SSNs). It also has six missile cruisers, which Russia sees as key elements in the restoration of the strategic bastion concept in the Arctic. The Northern Fleet has two flagships at its disposal, the largest nuclear icebreaker in the world, *Fifty Years of Victory*, and the main nuclear-powered guided missile cruiser (TAKR), *Peter the Great*. After the success of the *Peter the Great* around the world, in the fall of 2009, the Ministry of Defense announced that it would take two heavy nuclear-powered missile cruisers, the *Admiral Lazarev* and the *Admiral Nakhimov*, out of commission. The fourth ship in this class, the *Admiral Ushakov*, is currently undergoing modernization in Severodvinsk and may rejoin the active fleet. Currently, the *Admiral Kuznetsov* and the *Admiral Nakhimov* operate with the

Northern Fleet, each of which hosts 20 planes on board and 10 anti-submarine helicopters. Three new carriers are scheduled to be built and could be assigned to the Northern and the Pacific Fleets.[22] Another anti-missile cruiser, the *Vice-Admiral Kulakov*, only recently repaired, was integrated into the Northern Fleet in January 2010.[23] The naval aviation includes 200 combat planes and 50 helicopters. As with the other fleets, the Northern is severely lacking in costal ships and frigates able to conduct rapid intervention operations. Several are currently under construction, but the waiting times are problematic insofar as they reduce the fleet's protection capabilities.[24]

The older sea-based nuclear deterrent is in the process of being modernized. Today, the Russian Navy has six operational *Delta II* and six *Delta IV* strategic submarines that form the sea-based arm of its strategic nuclear deterrent. There are no plans to renovate the older *Delta III* class submarines, which were built during the 1980s, and they will be decommissioned in the coming decade. Six *Delta IV*s are being modernized: they will be equipped with a new sonar system and the new intercontinental ballistic missile (ICBM) Sineva, a third-generation liquid-propelled ICBM that entered service in 2007.[25] On October 11, 2008, during Northern Fleet military exercises, a Sineva rocket was fired from the nuclear submarine *Tula*, reaching its longest range yet, more than 11,500 kilometers.[26] Russia is planning to equip its *Delta IV* class submarines with at least 100 Sineva missiles, capable of carrying either four or ten nuclear warheads. This system enables missiles to be launched from under the ice, while remaining invisible to hostile observation satellites until the last moment.[27] The *Delta IV*'s operational life cycle should last until 2030. In January 2010, the Northern

Fleet received a vessel in this category called *Karelia*, which has been modernized to augment its tactical and technical capabilities and has been equipped with Sineva ballistic missiles.[28]

Many *Typhoon*-class strategic submarines — the world's largest, built in the 1980s — will also be re-armed to carry long-range cruise missiles. For the moment, only the *Dmitri Donskoy*, has been modernized and placed with the Northern Fleet. Today, it serves to conduct test firing for the Bulava system, a new generation solid-fuel SLBM built to avoid possible future U.S. ballistic missile defense (BMD) weapons, and which can travel more than 8,000 km. In the future, the *Typhoons* will be replaced with the new *Borey*-class nuclear-powered strategic submarines (Project 955). The first *Borey*-class submarine, the *Yuri Dolgoruky*, laid down in 1996, was placed with the Northern Fleet, while two others, the *Alexander Nevsky* and the *Vladimir Monomakh*, are being constructed at the Severodvinsk shipyard.[29] This new generation is almost undetectable at deep ocean depths and is used for multipurpose attacks. Thanks to its armaments, several types of cruise missiles and torpedoes, it will be able to carry out diverse missions, chase enemy aircraft carriers, and deliver massive missile strikes on coastal targets.[30] Eight of them are to be constructed by 2020 to replace the old *Delta III*, *Delta IV*, and *Typhoon*-class submarines.

However, a long string of unsuccessful test launches (six out of 11 have failed) has called into question the future of Russia's sea-based nuclear deterrent, as it is expected that the Bulava will be the only Russian sea-based ICBM after 2020-25. The former head of the research institute that designed the Bulava and Topol-M ballistic missiles, Yuri Solomonov, quit his post but stayed on as general designer of the project.[31] The costs for developing the Bulava and the *Borey* submarines take up a large part of the military budget, especially in times of economic crisis, and hamper any real reform of the army. Frozen after several failures, the tests are scheduled to recommence in the summer of 2010.[32] The Northern Fleet now finds itself in a vulnerable situation, since it is most directly affected by the repeated failures of the Bulava.

GROWING CIVIL-MILITARY COOPERATION

During the Soviet period, the hierarchy of priorities was devoid of all ambiguity. The army controlled those zones of the High North that were considered strategic, and companies wanting to exploit resources were subject to the good will of the Ministry of Defense. Thus in the 1980s, the idea of transforming Murmansk into a hub for Siberian oil bound for Western Europe was blocked by the army. Today, the situation has changed radically. In the 1990s, the army's weakness in comparison to economic groups has altered power relations, and despite the renaissance of the Russian military sector, for the Ministry of Defense there can be no possibility of setting aside the interests of companies like Gazprom, Lukoil, or Norilsk Nickel, which have powerful backing within the administration and can counterbalance the military point of view. These companies, whether public or private, and the army have come to the pragmatic conclusion that they depend on one another. The civil-military relationship is therefore in the process of changing profoundly, motivated not by reasons of principle concerning the control of civil society over the military, but by pragmatic economic interests that the army accepts or tries to turn to its own advantage.

Henceforth, the Northern Fleet is obliged to concern itself with protecting the growing economic interests of the Russian state in the Arctic. The proliferation of platforms in the sea, not to mention rigs, pipelines, and terminals on the coastlines, as well as the growth in maritime traffic, represents a new challenge for the army. There are many problems. Most oil facilities are not mobile, forcing the Ministry of Defense to put in place instruments assuring their protection in case of interstate conflict. Even if the Russian military considers these risks minimal, the potential for localized conflict must be taken into account. The securing of the platforms, pipelines, and ships against possible terrorist attacks accentuates the role of the special services in nontraditional threats. It entails a reorientation of defense around mobile units that are able to react rapidly and are equipped with high-technology hardware, all to the detriment of the traditional conception of armed forces that are numerically superior but slow to get moving. The possible presence of foreign companies in resource extraction also implies that non-Russian interests can be involved. In addition, the presence of a large number of tankers crossing sensitive zones can impede the circulation of military ships as well as submarines, which require space to maneuver and increase the risks of collision. Finally, the sonar emissions given off by the platforms and the oil industry interfere with military radar systems.[33]

Despite having to resolve these new complications, the Russian army has today become more comprehensive. Its new mission also gives it added weight with political authorities. The protection of Russian energy interests is likely to become one of the central elements in legitimacy for the Northern Fleet. In addition, this fleet is well-placed to garner material advantages. It benefits, for example, from cheaply priced fuel offered by extraction companies and gets its port infrastructure renovated at the latter's expense, without having to use up its own budget. On their side, statements from the extraction companies are increasingly pro-army, as a symbol of the renewal of Russian power. They are well aware that they need the support of the Northern Fleet to implement anti-terrorism protection systems, obtain the authorization to extract or to circulate in the sea, and access existing port infrastructures, fuel storage sites, and the large naval construction sites in the country's north. The main companies concerned — Gazprom, Lukoil, and Norilsk Nickel — have to contend, for example, not only with the lack of ice-free civil ports, but also with the absence of ports in deep water that are able to host 300,000-ton tankers. These companies would also like to take advantage of the military ships used for hydrographic and hydro-meteorological research, incorporating them in a sea rescue system of extreme logistical complexity.

Many examples attest to this rapprochement of interests. In 2005, the navy and Gazprom signed an agreement concerned with the latter's use of auxiliary ships, ports, and naval military sites, including setting up a security and rescue system and establishing maritime routes navigable by tankers, as well as establishing cooperation in terms of LNG.[34] This enabled Gazprom to construct an LNG processing plant for the Shtokman field in the closed town of Vidyayevo, a submarine base and garrison on the north shore of the Kola Peninsula. Further, in 2006, the Ministry of Defense agreed to provide the Russian industry with previously classified geological and topological maps. Since the 1990s, the army has allowed Lukoil arctic tankers to use a military fuel storage facility at Mokhnatkina Pakhta, near Murmansk, but denied the oil company the right to build a refinery, judging its location too close to military installations. One can therefore note how, despite robust rhetoric concerning the projection of power, Russian realities force Moscow to be much more pragmatic. The importance accorded to the energy sector means issues of the market and profitability tend to be ascendant over security decisions. The same economic logic is at play in the field of naval construction.

THE NEW STRATEGIES OF RUSSIAN NAVAL YARDS

The Russian Arctic program involves four major naval sites with historical links to the Northern Fleet: the two sites of St. Petersburg, Severnaia Verf and the Baltic factory, which are both partners and competitors, as well as the two Severodvinsk shipyards, Sevmash and Zvezdochka, situated about 30 km from Arkhangelsk. Moscow's desire to revive military naval construction can be realized only with the involvement of the civil sector. Since domestic capabilities are insufficient, the Russian merchant fleet orders 95 percent of its new ships from abroad and only 5 percent from Russian companies.[35] The market that has been lost by the Russian shipyards is thus immense, and with it the loss of knowledge. The case is similar for the fishing fleet, which wishes to renew its navigation hardware, half of which has exceeded the duration of its technical life. The most promising domain, however, is for the ships supporting the planned underwater mineral extraction endeavor on the Arctic shelf. For the Arctic and the Caspian seas, Russian companies claim to need 55 extraction platform, floating or submarine edifices, 85 transport ships, and 140 auxiliary ships by 2030.[36] The main naval military sites, then, have every interest in diversifying their orders by meeting the expectations of the civil fleet. Moreover, today they are part of the Ministry of Commerce and Economic Development, and not the Ministry of Defense.

The best example of this public-private cooperation in naval construction is the construction in St. Petersburg, by 2013 or 2014, of a new shipbuilding complex. Created for this purpose in 2004, the State Corporation OPK includes both the Severnaya Verf and Baltic shipyards, and the firm Aisberg (Iceberg), responsible for the design of new Arctic vessels. Both yards specialize in large nuclear vessels, such as *Fifty Years of Victory*, and have also recently built two diesel-electric icebreakers, including the *Moskva*, commissioned by Rosmorport. They are in charge of the construction of four Orlan nuclear cruisers and also await orders for large tankers. OPK cooperates closely with its private investment counterpart, OSK, which is the property of Mezhprombank and controlled by Senator Sergei Pugachev.[37] The total cost of the operation, estimated at 14 billion rubles (465 million dollars), gets state underwriting from Vneshtorgbank and Vneshekonombank. The flagship of this new site will be a floating bridge, capable of building oil tankers with a capacity of 300,000 tons and tankers carrying 150,000 to 215,000 m,[3] but also of responding to military orders.[38] The Russian government hopes to maintain the expertise of the Soviet era, acquire new technologies, especially by collaborating with Daewoo Shipbuilding and Marine Engineering (DSME), and to ensure its autonomy in terms of military shipbuilding so as not to depend on exports. Specializing in small coastal vessels, the new site could theoretically build 30 corvettes, 20 frigates, six escort squadrons, and 30 auxiliary vessels by 2020. For its part, Gazprom announced an order of eight gas carriers, the first of which will be operational in 2013 in order to move production from Shtokman.[39] The challenge of this new undertaking is immense in itself, compounded by the conflicting interests of the state and the OPK corporation, and competition between Severnaya Verf and Baltic, which continues to rage.[40]

By 2020, Russia hopes to double from seven to 14 the number of nuclear icebreakers capable of performing a complete circumnavigation of the North Pole. The Soviet nuclear icebreakers were built at the Baltic since 1974. The symbol is the icebreaker *Arktika*, which can ensure year-round navigation between Murmansk and Dudinka and extends the shipping season in Arctic regions. *Fifty Years of Victory*, left incomplete by the two St. Petersburg shipyards in 1993, was refueled with nuclear material in 2007. However, to circulate throughout the year along the polar route, Russia needs third-generation icebreakers that are more powerful and meet the expectations of large energy companies, which want icebreakers for geological research and exploitation of the seabed. The shipyards of St. Petersburg therefore specialize in the conquest program for the Arctic Sea. But the construction of new nuclear icebreakers is possible only with the participation of the Rosatom State Corporation (Russia's atomic energy state corporation). In April 2009, its director, Sergei Kiriyenko, announced that the level of government funding for building new nuclear icebreakers would total U.S. $57 million dollars from that year's federal budget and another $150 million from 2010-11. Cooperation with Kazakhstan in the nuclear industry meets the same objective. The joint Russian-

Kazakh venture Atomnye Stantsii (Atomic Stations) will manufacture VVER-300 reactors, intended not only for small nuclear power plants but also for the new Russian icebreakers. The partnership with Rosenergoatom includes as well the production by Severnaya Verf of spare parts for several new nuclear power plants ordered for Russia, India, and China.[41]

In Severodvinsk, the Sevmash shipyard has also had to reorient itself to civil construction. In the 1990s, military orders dropped 95 percent, and Sevmash was able to convert thanks to its dual-use technologies. In 2005, 33 percent of its orders came from the Ministry of Defense, 30 percent from the oil industry, and 25 percent from foreign companies. The company worked with the Indian Ministry of Defense in renovating and modernizing a cruiser aircraft carrier, the former *Admiral Gorshkov*, given to India in 2004, and building diesel-electric submarines for export through Rosoboronexport.[42] For the domestic military industry, Sevmash mainly deals with repairs to atomic cruisers like the *Admiral Rakhimov* and nuclear submarines like *Pantera*. Several ships and submarines decommissioned from the Russian army are used at Sevmash in cooperation programs with the United States and NATO.[43]

In terms of civilian seafaring, Sevmash renovated cruise ships like *Alushta*, transformed a submarine into a museum, and built a fish factory for the American company, Sea Wing, as well as several piers, two floating docks, barges, yachts, and frigates for the Swedish company, Promar. In 2004, the shipyard won the largest civil contract in its history for construction of ten 45,000-ton chemical tankers for the Norwegian company, Odfjell.[44] Gazprom has commissioned a floating platform for the extraction of oil in shallow water. The plant is also involved in the construction of several other types of platforms destined for the Pechora Sea or the Shtokman site. It collaborates with foreign companies such as Conoco, Total, and Halliburton, extracting the Ardalin and Khariagin deposits in the Nenets autonomous district. Finally, it provides materiel (pipelines) for oil transit to several national companies, such as Transneft, some Lukoil subsidiaries, Surgunneftergaz, Yugannedftegaz, and Yukos Service.[45] Lukoil expressed interest in the production of the shipyard, and Norilsk Nickel wishes to have its own fleet to move nickel extracted from Yenissei towards Murmansk without using the icebreaker shuttle transportation from the Murmansk Shipping Company.

The nearby plant Zvezdochka, the second industry in Severodvinsk, is more advanced in its civil conversion and even retrained its staff in activities totally unrelated to its primary expertise, for example, work on precious stones. To cope with the collapse of the domestic military command, since 1997 it has initiated cooperation with the Indian Ministry of Defense, which ordered the modernization and transformation of three diesel-electric Soviet submarines and two others. The Indian Navy recommissioned one of these, *Sindhuvidjay*, in 2007.[46] In 2003, Zvyozdochka won the right to independently conduct business operations abroad, and since 2008 has been authorized to renovate the 956th escort squadron. With this status, it sold over 30 million worth of military spare parts to foreign companies in 2009, mainly Indian and Chinese.[47]

It has also managed to penetrate the market of civilian seafaring. Since the early 1990s, it has won tenders from Dutch companies like Swets Shipping and Trading and received orders for a series of tugboats from

Damen Shipyards, and today works closely with Finnish and Norwegian companies. It built metal elements destined for Statoil, Kvaerner Oil and Gas, and Aker Solutions platforms, and expanded its partnership with Moss Maritime, a Norwegian leader in maritime technology. At home, Zvezdochka works with major energy companies and is also part of the Union of Producers of Oil and Gas Equipment. The plant is known for its construction of the 50010 trawler, considered the best in its class in terms of vessels produced in Russia. It is also one of the companies allowed to build new atomic vessels necessary to dominate the Arctic shelf. As such, it collaborates with Sevmash on several platform projects and on equipment for extracting oil, as well as with companies based in the Nenets district. Finally, in terms of military orders, it has built a series of carrier vessels for the shallow waters of Barents Sea, White Sea, and the Sea of Azov. Additionally, the border guard agency has commissioned a series of small patrol vessels for coastal surveillance.[48]

CONCLUSIONS

Russian ambitions in the Arctic are quite real, but they are still far from being realized. On the geopolitical level, Russia will have to contend with the United States, Canada, NATO, and the Nordic European states, which seek to affirm their own rights and statuses in the High North. From a strictly military point of view, the Northern Fleet has experienced major difficulties in modernizing and will have to resolve the questions emerging from the Bulava failures. In the economic sphere, the 2008-09 global crisis has put the brakes on major Russian projects to relaunch naval construction. From a technical perspective, Gazprom and other Russian companies have not yet mastered the requisite cutting-edge offshore technologies and will have to continue to work closely with foreign partners. Despite its Soviet legacy in the Arctic, Russia does not yet have sufficient capability to dominate that region. The Russian port system is in bad condition, and its polar stations, meteorological and hydrological satellites, and securitization of its navigation systems are not yet operational. Of the country's 14 hydrographic ships, 11 have been in operation for over 25 years, and more than 17,000 km of Arctic coastlines are reportedly not covered by radio, with Russia having to buy information from the United States and Canada.[49] Plans for power projection are therefore far removed from actual capacity to act. Yet, one cannot help noting the extent of Russian interest in the Arctic. The dynamic of military renewal in the region is based on real economic interests, in which the civil overrides the military, and pragmatic issues such as technical capability counterbalance nationalist escalation. Even if, for the time being, the potential for international cooperation between the Arctic littoral states does not have great resonance in Russia, the technological and financial difficulties faced in High North exploitation could serve to change this situation. In any case, the Kremlin is not interested in sacrificing its future as a great power in the name of international cooperation in the absence of negotiations, meaningful discussions, or at least symbolic compensations.

ENDNOTES - CHAPTER 3

1. R. Boswell, "Arctic sea route to be renamed 'Canadian Northwest Passage'," *Canwest News Service*, December 3, 2009, available from *www.vancouversun.com/news/Arctic+route+renamed +Canadian+Northwest+Passage/2300092/story.html*.

2. P. Baev, "Russia's Race for the Arctic and the New Geopolitics of the North Pole," *Jamestown Occasional Papers*, October 2007.

3. A. Chilingarov, "Arktika – nash rodnoi krai," *Regnum.ru*, July 7, 2007, available from *www.regnum.ru/news/867158.html*.

4. "SShA i Rossiia razdeliaiut Arktiku," *Pogranichnik.ru*, January 14, 2009, available from *forum.pogranichnik.ru/index.php? showtopic=10737*.

5. J. MacCannon, *Red Arctic: Polar Exploration and the Myth of the North in the Soviet Union, 1932-1939*, Oxford, UK: Oxford University Press, 1998.

6. K. Bozena Zysk, "Russian Military Power and the Arctic," *Russian Foreign Policy*, Brussels, Belgium: The EU-Russia Center, No. 8, 2008, pp. 80-86; K. Bozena Zysk, "Russia and the High-North. Security and Defense Perspectives," *Security Prospects in the High-North: Geostrategic Thaw or Freeze?* Rome, Italy: NATO Defence College, May 2009, pp. 102-129.

7. "Vystuplenie na zasedanii Soveta Bezopasnosti, 'O zashchite natsional'nykh interesov Rossii v Arktike'," *Kremlin.ru*, September 17, 2008, available from *www.kremlin.ru/transcripts/1433*.

8. "Northern Fleet," *Global Security*, no date, *www.globalsecurity.org/military/world/russia/mf-north.htm*.

9. "Rossiia usilivaet voenno-morskoe prisutstvie v Arktike," *Natsional'naia bezopasnost'*, July 18, 2008, available from *national-safety.ru/n18964*.

10. "Samolety-raketonostsy VVP RF vedut patrulirovanie v raionakh Arktiki," *RIA Novosti*, July 9, 2008, available from *www.militaryparitet.com/teletype/data/ic_teletype/2746/*.

11. "General Shamanov: Rossiia gotovitsia k voine za Arktiku," *Polit.ru*, June 24, 2008, available from *www.polit.ru/news/2008/06/24/getready.html*.

12. V. Shurygin, "Voina y poroga," *Shurigin live journal*, March 31, 2009, available from *shurigin.livejournal.com/174272. html?page=5.*

13. "Rossiia sozdaet otdel'nuiu gruppirovku voisk v Arktike," *Grani.ru*, March 27, 2009, available from *grani.ru/Politics/ Russia/m.149100.html.*

14. N. Petrov, "The Russian Navy Gets Ambitious," *RIA Novosti*, August 01, 2007, available from *www.spacedaily.com/reports/ The_Russian_Navy_Gets_Ambitious_999.html.*

15. Z. Barany, *Democratic Breakdown and the Decline of the Russian Military*, Princeton, NJ: Princeton University Press, 2007.

16. M. Sieff, "Makarov pledges to complete Russian army reform by 2012," *UPI.com*, February 9, 2009, available from *www.upi. com/Business_News/Security-Industry/2009/02/09/Makarov-pledges-to-complete-Russian-army-reform-by-2012/UPI-95081234222215/.*

17. V. Patrushev, "Flotu neobkhodimy remont i modernizatsiia," *Nezavisimaia gazeta*, October 06, 2006, available from *nvo. ng.ru/armament/2006-10-06/6_flot.html.*

18. "Voenno-morskoi flot RF nuzhdaetsia v rezkom, mnogokratnom uvelichenii denezhnykh sredstv dlia ego razvitiia-admiral Kravchenko," *Flot.com*, February 26, 2008, available from *flot. com/news/vpk/index.php?ELEMENT_ID=5354.*

19. "Russia: Northern Fleet,"Monterey, CA: Center for Nonproliferation Studies, 2002, available from *www.nti.org/db/nisprofs/ russia/naval/nucflt/norflt/norflovr.htm.*

20. D. Rudolph, "The Arctic Military Environmental Cooperation (AMEC) Program's role in the management of spent fuel from decommissioned nuclear submarines," *Scientific and Technical Issues in the Management of Spent Fuel of Decommissioned Nuclear Submarines*, Dordrecht, The Netherlands: NATO Science Series II, Mathematics, Physics and Chemistry, 2006.

21. "Severnyi flot," *Vlast'* , No 7 (760), February 25, 2008, available from *www.kommersant.ru/doc.aspx?DocsID=856043.*

L15-L18

22. J. W. Kipp, "The Russian Navy Recalibrates its Oceanic Ambitions," *Free Republic*, October 30, 2009, available from *www. freerepublic.com/focus/news/2375147/posts*.

23. "Bol'shoi protivolodochnyi korabl' Severnogo Flota *Vitse-admiral Kulakov* vyidet na khodovye ispytaniia," *Severnyi Flot*, January 14, 2010, available from *www.severnyflot.ru/news. php?extend.1969*.

24. "VMF Rossii popolnitsia novymi korabliami," *Severnyi Flot*, January 11, 2010, available from *www.severnyflot.ru/news. php?extend.1961*.

25. "State-of-the-art nuclear submarines to the Russian Navy," *Barents Observer*, June 19, 2009, available from *www.barentsobserver.com/state-of-the-art-nuclear-submarines-to-the-russian-navy.4608935-58932.html*.

26. "Sineva extended range launch," *Russianforces.org*, October 11, 2008, available from *russianforces.org/blog/2008/10/sineva_extended_range_launch.shtml*.

27. P. Felgenhauer, "The Bulava SLBM and the US-Russian Arms Talks," *Eurasia Daily Monitor*, Vol. 6, No. 232, December 17, 2009.

28. "APL Kareliia 22 ianvaria budet peredana VMF Rossii," *Severnyi Flot*, January 11, 2010, available from *www.severnyflot.ru/news.php?extend.1964*.

29. Felgenhauer, "The Bulava SLBM and the US-Russian Arms Talks."

30. Petrov, "The Russian Navy Gets Ambitious."

31. "Solomonov to keep working on Bulava development-Roscosmos," *RIA Novosti*, September 15, 2009, available from *en.rian.ru/mlitary_news/20090915/156136868.html*.

32. "New Bulava tests this summer," *Barents Observer*, January 11, 2010, available from *www.barentsobserver.com/new-bulava-tests-this-summer.4683771-116321.html*.

33. For more details, see K. Atland, "Russia's Northern Fleet and the Oil Industry—Rivals or Partners? A Study of Civil-Military Relations in the Post-Cold War Arctic," *Armed Forces & Society*, Vol. 35, No. 2, 2009, pp. 362-384.

34. "Gazprom and RF Navy Ink Cooperation Agreement," *Gazprom Press Release*, November 24, 2005, available from *old.gazprom.ru/eng/news/2005/11/18373.shtml.*

35. "Sudostroitel'nyi kompleks OPK gotov k uchastiiu v gosudarstvenno-chastnom partnerstve," *Okean Pribor*, May 15, 2008, available from *shipbuilding.ru/rus/news/russian/2008/05/15/opk/.*

36. "Ob osnovykh napravleniiakh gosudarstvennoi promyshlennoi politiki i ee realizatsiia v sudostroitel'noi otrasl," *Fishnews.ru*, February 15, 2007, available from *www.fishnews.ru/news/1485.*

37. "Sudostroitel'nyi kompleks OPK gotov k uchastiiu v gosudarstvenno-chastnom partnerstve."

38. "Dominanta gosudarstvennogo podkhoda," *Arsenal. Voenno-promyslennoe obozrenie*, No. 4, 2008, available from *rusarm.com/arhiv/n4_2008/dominanta_gosudarstvennogo_podhoda/.*

39. See OPK website, available from *www.opk.ru/shipbuilding/.*

40. A. Gritskova and E. Kiseleva, "Ot Baltzavoda otchalil gendirektor," *Kommersant*, No. 191 (4008), October 21, 2008, available from *www.kommersant.ru/pda/kommersant.html?id=1044809.*

41. "Chuzhie proschety ispravit OTsK," *Portnews.ru*, May 21, 2008, available from *portnews.ru/comments/286/?print=1.*

42. See Sevmash website, available from *www.sevmash.ru/?id=2830&lg=ru.*

43. *Ibid.*

44. *Ibid.*

45. *Ibid.*

46. *Ibid.*

47. "Tsentr sudoremonta Zvezdochka postavit v 2009 g. inoza-kazchikam zapchasti dlia remonta voennykh korablei na summu 30 millionov dollarov," *Korabel.ru*, September 7, 2009, available from *www.korabel.ru/news/comments/tsentr_sudoremonta_zvezdoch-ka_postavit_v_2009_godu_inozakazchikam_zapchasti_dlya_remonta_voennih_korabley_na_summu_30_mln_dol.html*.

48. See Zvezdochka's website, available from *www.star.ru/in-dex.php?page=130*.

49. "Rossiia usilivaet voenno-morskoe prisutstvie v Arktike."

CHAPTER 4

THE EVOLVING ARCTIC SECURITY ENVIRONMENT: AN ASSESSMENT

Katarzyna Zysk[1]

INTRODUCTION

The Arctic[2] is no longer like we used to know it, a politically and economically remote backwater of international relations. Climate changes in the region, proceeding at the fastest pace and in the severest form on the globe, generate a chain of reactions affecting the region's geopolitical landscape. As the ice sheet retreats, new opportunities emerge alongside new security challenges and threats.

However, early enthusiastic predictions about an unprecedented commercial bonanza in the region based on an increased accessibility to abundant natural riches and opening of attractive new shipping lanes have turned out to be too optimistic. Likewise, predictions about a military conflict in the region, often portrayed as an outcome of a Hobbesian "free for all" for Arctic energy resources, is proving to be largely overstated.[3] The increased international interest in the region in recent years has led rather to intensification of political processes, in particular among the countries known as the Arctic 5 (Canada, Denmark [Greenland], Norway, Russia, and the United States). One of the outcomes of the strengthened dialogue was the preliminary agreement between Russia and Norway, signed in March 2010 after 40 years of negotiations, on delimitation of the resource-rich Barents

Sea.[4] Nevertheless, there are a number of challenges deriving from transformations in the Arctic's natural and, in consequence, its strategic environment, and it is still not clear how various possible scenarios will ultimately play out.

The state of the Arctic security environment is analyzed, with focus on economic, jurisdictional, political, and security processes in the region. Particular attention is devoted to the role of the Russian Federation, as the country that holds the key to political development in the Arctic in the decades to come. There are several factors that contribute to that. Russia is one of the most determined Arctic players, with high ambitions for development of the region. Apart from being the largest polar state from the geographical point of view, Russia defines the region as crucial for the country's economy as a future main base for strategic natural resources.[5] At the same time, despite radical changes in the Arctic security environment after the end of the Cold War, the region has never ceased to play a central role in Russian military strategic thinking and the country's defense policy.

BACKGROUND: REEMERGENCE OF THE ARCTIC

With the end of the Cold War, the Arctic has quickly lost its geopolitical significance as one of its major fronts, characterized by the greatest concentration of the Soviet Union's nuclear forces and hosting the strongest part of its Navy. This concept was embodied in the North in Admiral Sergei Goshkov's concept of a strategic bastion. However, since the beginning of the new millennium and especially over the last 5 years, the Arctic has begun attracting international attention again. Among the main factors that turned the world's eyes toward the region was its representation as one of the most promising new energy frontiers on the globe. Much of the focus has been generated by the U.S. Geological Survey's World Petroleum Assessment from 2000, which was widely interpreted as attributing 25 percent of the world's recoverable undiscovered energy resources to the Arctic.[6] The Middle East's instability and high gas and oil prices from 2004 to the first half of 2008 helped galvanize interest in the vast, untapped Arctic hydrocarbon deposits.[7] Predictions about an upcoming "Arctic Gold Rush,"[8] together with alarmist assessments by a large share of the news media, as well as some experts and academics who portrayed intrastate relations in this region with unresolved border lines as virtually chaotic and governed by realpolitik, have also contributed to much of the international interest.

Furthermore, a more assertive Russian stance, emphasized by a systematic increase in military activity in the North's air and maritime domains since 2007, as well as tough responses to these moves from the other polar states, have fanned the flames. The sometimes belligerent Russian rhetoric and behavior have contributed to the perception of Russia as the "wild card" in the Arctic strategic equation. The 2007 flag-planting episode by the Russian submarine crew on the seabed under the North Pole—an act with no legal implications and whose importance was grossly exaggerated—has fueled speculation about an impending new Cold War with an Arctic epicenter.

The focus on the Arctic has been further prompted by extraordinary climatic deviations in the region from apparent historic norms. Global warming has particularly profound consequences in the Arctic because in a global context its effects amplify at higher latitudes.[9] Arctic warming is thus predicted to be more than twice the global average (3 to 4 degrees Celsius) in the next 50 years.[10] As a result, the ice cap is shrinking and thinning, thus altering the ratio in favor of younger first-year ice over multiyear ice cover that has survived at least one summer melt season.[11] In 2007 the Arctic sea ice, monitored by satellite for 3 decades, reached a record minimum.[12] In some projections, Arctic late-summer sea ice will virtually disappear by the latter part of the 21st century.[13] Other model simulations suggest that these estimates may be too conservative, and an ice-free summer in the region could possibly arrive as early as in 2030.[14]

There has been a growing awareness around the world that the emergence of an ice-diminished Arctic will have both regional and global implications over the shorter and longer term. The increased international interest has resulted in reports, policies, or strategies drawn for the region not only by the Arctic littoral states, but also by international organizations and actors relatively distant from the region and seemingly with no direct interest. They have been attracted by the promise of economic opportunities and/or concerned about potential negative consequences of these transformations.

Among the most active states that have contributed to the growing international interest in the region are Norway and Russia. In 2005 the Norwegian government designated the High North[15] to be a strategic priority and presented in the following year a comprehensive strategy for the region.[16] Russia's increased focus on the Arctic has resulted in an updated regional policy document endorsed in September 2008.[17] Also, the other polar states have expressed their own growing interest in Arctic affairs.[18] The region has been a particularly salient issue in Canadian domestic politics and the country's foreign relations, in particular with the other polar rim states.[19] Although the Arctic is still a rather peripheral issue in the United States, the Obama administration focused on the problem of climate change and improving relations with Russia, with consequent steadily increased attention to the region.[20]

Elsewhere, the European Security and Defense Assembly (WEU) has explored developments in the Arctic and in November 2008 recommended that the European Union (EU) and the North Atlantic Treaty Organization (NATO) include the region in their strategies, including attention to the security consequences of climate change and the receding ice.[21] Sharing this concern, NATO leaders convened in January 2009 to discuss security prospects and the role of the Alliance in the High North, while the EU has taken steps towards drawing a comprehensive Arctic policy.[22]

Furthermore, even Asian countries—notably China but also India, Japan, and South Korea—have turned their attention northward. China and South Korea, along with the EU and Italy, have sought a permanent observer status in the Arctic Council, although so far unsuccessfully, and their applications will not be reviewed before the Council's next meeting this year. China is slowly but steadily recognizing the commercial and strategic opportunities that may arise from an ice-free Arctic, first and foremost being shortened trade routes to European and North American markets and possible access to untapped natural resources to fuel China's economy.[23] The Chinese government has allocated extra resources for construction of a new high-tech polar expedition icebreaker and is investing in Arctic research.[24] Similarly to India, China has established a permanent research station in Ny-Ålesund at the Norwegian Svalbard archipelago to enhance understanding of the evolving Arctic natural environment.

Even though much of the international focus on the Arctic has been generated by exaggerated assessments of economic opportunities and security threats, there is no doubt that multidimensional transformations taking place in the region have the potential to influence world affairs in a spectrum of areas. The following sections analyze processes within the main spheres that have brought the Arctic forth as a geopolitical issue, namely, energy and maritime transport, legal disputes, and security dynamics.

ARCTIC ENERGY

The Arctic's oil and gas potential has been widely discussed. The 2008 Circum-Arctic Resource Appraisal by the U.S. Geological Survey (USGS) portrayed the region as one of the biggest unexplored energy regions in the world. According to this study, the Arctic embraces as much as 22 percent of the undiscovered resources in the world, located mostly offshore (84 percent), and including 13 percent of oil, 30 percent of natural gas, and 20 percent of natural gas liquids.[25]

However, the USGS emphasizes that low data density and high geological uncertainty affects the accuracy of estimates of the region's energy reserves. More research will be necessary to define the resource potential more accurately. Nevertheless, the Arctic stands out as one of the most promising energy venues in the world.

According to the USGS, the fact that most of the Arctic gas and oil potential is in the Russian sector makes that country a key player within regional energy extraction, particularly in case of the projected undiscovered natural gas. More than 70 percent of these resources is estimated to be in Western Siberia and East Barents basins, in addition to Arctic Alaska.[26] According to official Russian sources, 80 percent of known Russian gas reserves and 90 percent of hydrocarbon deposits on the Russian continental shelf are in the Arctic, 66.5 percent of which is located in the Barents and Kara Seas.[27] Today the Russian regions north of the Arctic Circle produce as much as 20 percent of the gross domestic product, 11 percent of gross national income, and 22 percent of total Russian exports.[28] Not surprisingly, the Russian leadership emphasizes the importance of the region to the country's wealth and competitiveness in the global marketplace as a major source of revenue crucial for national energy security, with a direct bearing on Russia's international standing.[29] According to key policy documents recently adopted by Russia, including the Energy Strategy, for the period up to 2030, development of energy fields in the Arctic seas and in the Russian northern regions is to play a stabilizing role by stemming a possible decline in gas and oil production in Western Siberia expected between 2015 and 2030.[30] Hence, one of the main goals of Russian Arctic policy is to increase extraction of natural resources in that region.[31]

Despite the fact that large parts of the Russian government and population maintain conservative attitudes toward the problem of global warming, in particular toward the role of the human factor, they expect at the same time that the observed climatic aberrations may create new opportunities for development of certain parts of the national economy, including in the northern regions. Hesitant about tackling climate change until recently, Russia is devoting more attention to its expected effects. In December 2009, prior to the United Nations (UN) Climate Change Conference in Copenhagen (COP15), President Dmitrii Medvedev signed a doctrinal statement on climate change. The document points out that much of Russian territory is located within the region undergoing the strongest effects of the climatic transformations (both observed and forecasted).[32] Among their expected negative implications, the document lists an increase in health problems and death rates in certain parts of the population; increased frequency and intensity of extreme floods and fires; melting of the permafrost; destabilization in ecological balance; and geopolitical tensions caused by migrations.[33] However, despite these challenges and threats, at the same time the Russian authorities expect a number of benefits deriving from these dynamics, including improved ice conditions for Arctic Sea transport and easier access to and development of mineral and energy resources on the continental shelf.[34]

The projected growth in global demand for energy, together with diminishing reserves in fields currently under exploitation, may accelerate calls for extraction of Arctic gas and oil. Nevertheless, their future development is characterized by high uncertainty and will be an outcome of a number of factors, including energy prices, technological advances, production from other energy regions, and developments in the field of alternative fuels.

Extremely harsh climatic conditions in the Arctic constitute enormous technological challenges for the petroleum industry and, together with long distances to necessary infrastructure, make the Arctic a high-cost region for extraction. The industry will also have to face environmental concerns, particularly in the case of oil-spill accidents in the Arctic and elsewhere. The catastrophic oil spill from an offshore drilling rig in the Gulf of Mexico in April 2010, potentially surpassing the damage of the formerly worst oil spill in history by the Exxon *Valdez* tanker in 1989, has already raised calls for a permanent ban on offshore drilling, and strengthened opposition against opening the territories near Norway's Lofoten and Vesteraalen islands for the oil industry.[35] New technologies for spill response and other crisis management, disaster relief, and search and rescue capacities suitable for polar conditions, will have to be provided to enable these activities to continue. Among decisive factors in investors' assessments will be technological progress and energy prices. Recently, this correlation has been confirmed in developments in the Russian Shtokman offshore gas project in the Barents Sea.[36] Due to the negative impact of the global financial crisis on domestic and foreign gas demand and relatively low energy prices, the project has been delayed.[37] Russia has encountered a similar problem in its largest gas field on the Yamal Peninsula, Bovanenkovo, which had to be postponed until 2012.[38]

Other important factors that will have an impact on the future of the Arctic as a new energy frontier are developments in the field of increased energy efficiency and alternative fuels. Both may reduce energy prices and growth in demand for Arctic gas and oil, as well as reshuffling the map of the world energy market. Development of commercial unconventional natural gas (UNG) resources, such as shale gas from rock formations, particularly in the United States, is one such example. Recent technological advances have made exploitation of shale gas—previously considered too difficult and too expensive—now easier and more cost-effective.[39] Shale gas extraction has spread in the United States, transforming the North American natural gas market by leading to oversupply of natural gas. Together with access to cheap liquefied natural gas (LNG) from Qatar, it has contributed to a decrease in the price of gas in this region.[40] Although reliance on shale gas is still in a very early phase in other parts of the globe, exploration projects are under way, including Europe.[41]

Such developments may result in aggravating the uncertainty regarding the balance between supply and demand and lead to a shrinking of current markets and lower gas prices. As a result, they may reduce incentives driving production of Arctic energy deposits, where significant and expensive investments are necessary.[42] According to Deputy Minister for Natural Resources Sergei Donskoi, due to the delays in development of Arctic offshore fields, Russia has already lost the U.S. energy market for the gas from Shtokman, and risks losing the European market as well.[43]

The Russian government has been taking steps to address these problems. It emphasizes the need to intensify geological surveys in the Arctic seas in order to more accurately define the energy potential and thus attract investors. In 2010, all money from the federal budget allocated for geological study of the Arctic shelf was used to examine just the Arctic seas.[44] The amounts in question are, however, relatively small, reportedly up to 30 times less than those projected by Gazprom and Rosneft before they were cut by 20–30 percent due to the financial crisis.[45] Hardship in the Russian economy contributes to strengthening the modernization and reform forces in Russia. The Ministry for Natural Resources and Ecology, as well as the Ministry of Energy, has spoken in favor of liberalization of access to the offshore energy fields, which are considered an exclusive state monopoly.[46] Minister for Natural Resources Yurii Trutnev acknowledged, though, that this idea still faces opposition in certain parts of the Russian government.[47]

Although the Arctic in general, and the Russian sector in particular, stands out as a promising energy venue, the pace of exploration of offshore fields is likely to remain limited in the immediate future, together with the human activity and security challenges related to it. Yet, the expected increase in energy consumption worldwide may be generating interest for the Arctic riches, particularly in energy-thirsty economies such as China. Although, as argued above, there is a range of factors militating against interest in energy production in the Arctic, the future of those factors is also characterized by high uncertainty.

MARITIME TRANSPORT

Another broadly discussed implication of the retreating ice in the Arctic Ocean is the possibility of opening new Arctic maritime transport route for world trade. The opened passages promise to cut transit distances by thousands of miles between some of the major world markets, making the Arctic an attractive alternative to current trade routes.

The Northern Sea Route (NSR, also called the Northeast Passage) along the Russian Arctic shoreline has virtually always been closed to navigation, at least since 1553. Since 2005, however, it has been open each summer.[48] In 2009 two German ships made the first commercial voyage ever through the passage, with minimal assistance by Russian icebreakers.[49]

The Northwest Passage (NWP) in the Canadian Arctic is likely to be the last route to open for commercial traffic according to climatic models, but in the future it too may offer shorter maritime transport routes. A third possibility is a passage directly across the Polar Sea, considered economically and politically more viable than both the NWP and the NSR although probably the last to be open due to climatic conditions.[50]

Nevertheless, there is a host of technical and economic factors that have to be clarified and/or overcome before new trade routes through the polar region become possible and commercially competitive. Although the Arctic passages offer a considerable shortcut for shipping between ports located in northern parts of Europe, Asia, and North America as compared to routes using the Suez or Panama Canals, the savings in distance may not necessarily translate into savings in time. The high costs of operations in Arctic seas and a range of limitations and uncertainties such as slower sailing speed may outweigh potential benefits, limiting the Arctic's commercial shipping potential.[51]

Various studies show that the Arctic routes may be shorter, but not necessarily faster.[52] Drifting ice, extreme temperatures, and difficult weather conditions, as well as polar night and poorly mapped waters, are among factors that are likely to slow navigation and thus lengthen transit time. Consequently, the Arctic passages will not necessarily result in fuel, emissions, and manpower savings.[53] Moreover, the ships will have reduced cargo carrying capacity, because some of the Arctic straits are shallow. Nor can the vessels be wider than the icebreakers which will have to be used to open their way through the ice at times. The ships will also be more expensive as their hulls will have to be strengthened to withstand the impact of ice. Together with higher insurance premiums necessitated by the higher risk of sailing in Arctic waters, transport costs might actually rise. Shipowners and operators may also be discouraged by an inability to maintain all-year operations. Finally, it will be impossible to predict exactly when and for how long the passages will be open.[54]

All that said, the routes may still be attractive and more stable than waters in the south facing challenges connected to piracy and the associated rapid rise in insurance costs.[55] Once the polar routes are established, there will be an impact on international relations by redistributing profits among countries and regions, with some gaining and some losing.[56]

Russia is among the actors likely to profit most from an open Arctic in the context of maritime transport. As a country "owning" the NSR, Russia will control new passages of world trade and economics. According to Russian regulations, which may or may not prevail, all vessels intending to enter the NSR must give notification in advance to the Russian authorities, submit an application for guidance, and pay a fee for icebreaker assistance.[57] The Russian government has expressed strong interest in promotion of the route for international shipping as a central element in maritime connections between Europe and Asia, all under Russian jurisdiction.[58]

The NSR also appears as an alternative for the transport of Russian Arctic gas and oil. Shipping through the NRS westward from the Barents and Kara Seas is expected to increase in the coming years simply as a corollary of the development of Russian energy reserves.[59] Russia also plans to ship energy products though this channel eastward to Asia. In the summer of 2010, the first ever oil tanker has been scheduled to sail the entire NSR from the Varandey oil terminal on the Pechora Sea coast to Japan. The Sovcomflot, Russia's largest state-owned maritime shipping company specializing in petroleum and LNG shipping, has announced plans to carry out shipping through the NSR from the yet-to-be-built LNG plant on the Yamal Peninsula to Asian markets.[60] According to some analysts, Russia aims at increasing its share in export revenues in the future to preserve the state's income.[61] From this perspective, the NSR may constitute an important element in Russia's energy security, understood primarily as security of energy delivery.

However, in this case a variety of conditions has to be met in order to satisfy requirements of increased maritime activity. As Russian authorities themselves note, restructuring the volume of maritime freight through the NSR requires refurbishing the neglected infrastructure, building modern harbors, and establishing a system of communications managment. To secure the Euro-Asian transit, Russia also has to provide support and crisis management capabilities and must rejuvenate its aging nuclear-powered icebreaker fleet.[62] Maintaining the icebreaker capability will be crucial for the future of the NSR and economic development of the Arctic. A long-term plan for construction of new third-generation icebreakers was drafted by the Russian State Nuclear Energy Corporation in 2009. However, as with many other ambitious plans for the Arctic, its implementation has been delayed due to the financial constraints caused by the global economic crisis.[63]

In the short term, shipping activities in the Arctic are expected to increase as a result of the exploitation of the Russian energy deposits in the High North. Together with a likely surge in maritime research and other scientific activities—as well as Arctic tourism and to a certain degree the fishing that will follow changing migratory patterns of fish stocks—these developments will provide regional economic benefits. But any large-scale trans-Arctic shipping lies in the long term, and it has an uncertain outcome.

LEGAL ISSUES AND CONFLICT POTENTIAL

Prospects for economic development in the Arctic have shed new light on existing legal disputes in the region. Most of the public attention has been attracted by the potential overlapping territorial claims between Denmark and Canada on the one hand, and Russia on the other. These claims refer to parts of the Arctic continental shelf around the North Pole. Speculation about the potential for conflict has been based mainly on the assumption that a struggle for gas and oil in the disputed areas may lead to the use of military force. The basic flow of the argument stems from the fact that most of the energy wealth is located in economic zones subject to the unquestioned national jurisdiction of the Arctic Ocean states.[64] According to the USGS study, the region around the North Pole and middle of the Arctic Basin is not among areas with a high probability of finding petroleum.[65]

The legal process of extending outer limits of continental shelves beyond 200 nautical miles within the framework of the multilateral legal regime of the UN Convention on the Law of the Sea will take years before any conclusion about sovereignty over the Arctic seabed is reached. Both Canada and Denmark have not submitted their claims yet. Russia submitted its first request in 2001, but the Commission on the Limits of the Continental Shelf requested more evidence.[66] The Russian authorities have given a high priority to the task of defining the limits of its Arctic zone, which is planned to be accomplished by 2015.[67] The question of how Russia may react in case of a denial of its claim to an extended continental shelf remains open. It should be remembered, though, that Russia already exercises unquestioned control over enormous energy deposits in the Arctic. According to Minister Trutnev, in today's terms, Russia has sufficient reserves to cover production for the next 25–35 years, and it does not include newly discovered reserves.[68] Although one can and should assume that the country will strive to expand its sovereignty over as much of the new territories and resources as possible, just as the other Arctic states will, Russia is not pressed for time.

In addition to the process of extending continental shelves, there are three remaining unsettled maritime borders in the Arctic. As pointed out earlier, one of the most problematic legal issues in the Arctic and in Norwegian-Russian relations — the delimitation of the Barents Sea — has been solved. Two remaining border issues concern areas with a high probability of finding hydrocarbon deposits.[69] Among them is the Canadian-U.S. disagreement in the Beaufort Sea. The problem has been, however, subjected to a diplomatic process. Moreover, despite existing frictions, a military confrontation for territory between NATO nations seems highly remote. The U.S.-Russian dispute about a maritime border in the Bering and Chukchi Seas has already been framed in an agreed document and remains to be ratified by the State Duma.[70] The third border dispute, between Canada and Denmark, concerns Hans Island—a small uninhabitable 1.3 square kilometer knoll in the center of the Kennedy Channel of the Nares Strait. Despite its potential for attracting the attention of the news media over occasional spectacular gestures by both countries, this disagreement is the least prone to spur any military confrontation.

Certain challenges are related to Norway's relations with other states, Russia in particular, in the 200 nautical mile Fishery Protection Zone (FPZ) established by Norwegian authorities around the Svalbard archipelago in 1977.[71] Norway has been granted unquestioned sovereignty over these islands by the Treaty of 1920, but the treaty has granted to all signatory states, currently 39 nations including Russia, the right to undertake economic activity at the archipelago.[72] According to Norway, the treaty does not apply to the economic zone around it; the other countries beg to disagree. Due to the different views on the geographical scope of the treaty, Norway has chosen to establish the fishing zone rather than a full economic zone. Apart from Norway, Russia is the other major actor with a significant settlement on Svalbard and economic activity in the FPZ, never acknowledged by Russia officially. Nonetheless, despite sporadic tensions based mainly on access to fish resources, Russia has in practice respected the Norwegian jurisdiction. Apart from good bilateral relations between these two countries, strengthened by multilevel cooperation along a spectrum of areas, a stabilizing factor is that both states are interested in preserving the status quo in the region since revision of the archipelago's legal regime may throw open Pandora's Box to other claimants, threatening Russia's privileged position, as well as Norway's jurisdiction in the questioned area.[73]

Two other issues in the Arctic concern the legal status of the NWP and the NSR. Canada considers the NWP to be internal waters, while the United States chooses to see the passage as an international strait and thus subject to the right of transit passage. A similar problem affects the legal status of certain parts of the NSR. Russia defines the NSR as a national transportation route under Russia's jurisdiction.[74] Navigation through this sailing channel, which must comply with Russian laws, also includes passage through straits within and between the four Russian Arctic archipelagos, Vilkitski, Shokalski, Dmitri Laptev, and Sannikov. Russia designates the straits as part of its internal waters, while the United States has explicitly labeled them as international.[75]

However, the jurisdictional disputes in the Arctic are subject to international law, which limits the room for military conflict.[76] The region has a stable legal regime based on principles of international cooperation to which all five polar states have committed themselves. They have agreed to regulate remaining disagreements within the legal framework and through negotiations.[77] In the case of Russia, the cooperative and pragmatic approach has been emphasized in its key documents and political declarations.[78] Russia has repeatedly underlined its belief that the Arctic is not a zone of potential conflict and that Russia will be a reliable partner in the region.[79]

Likewise, the political and economic usefulness of escalating legal disagreements to a significant interstate war in lieu of pressing for the preferred legal solution seems unlikely. It would involve high political and material costs likely to outweigh any conceivable gains by destabilizing the region and making extraction of energy and other economic activities more difficult, if possible at all. Such a "solution" is thus likely to defeat the purpose of operating in the area.

A further consideration is that the Arctic is an environment of extreme operational challenges, even for armed forces with long-standing Arctic experience. As put by Canada's Chief of Defence Staff General Walter Natynczyk: "If someone were to invade the Canadian Arctic, my first task would be to rescue them."[80] Dialogue, cooperation, and stability, all necessary to address new emerging security challenges, may further strengthen the sense of cooperation.[81] Simply put, keeping tension low is mutually profitable for all parties involved, including Russia.

Security assessments, however, must always give a nod to worst-case scenarios, not just to the most probable outcomes, in order to ensure acceptable results under all realizable conditions.[82] The potential for conflict in the Arctic, although unlikely today, cannot be fully ruled out. There is a possibility that disagreement over particular political issues, intertwined with identity issues and domestic politics, could take on a more confrontational course, creating serious tensions and sparking local episodes based, for instance, on access to fish resources, despite the original benign intentions of parties involved.[83] The increased strategic importance of the Arctic and its stronger connection with global affairs may also render it more vulnerable to potential spill-over effects from crises or conflicts in other parts of the world. Any hypothetical conflict in the region today is more likely to be heated up outside the region than inside.

For the present, developments in Arctic security will depend to a high degree on the general, overarching framework formed by Russia's relations with the United States and NATO and, in the future, with other possible major stakeholders in the region, such as the Asian countries.

SECURITY DYNAMICS AND THE RUSSIA FACTOR

While an armed confrontation in the Arctic appears unlikely in the current political and economic constellation, the physical transformation of the region and potential future surge in human activities will call for capabilities to assure safety and security of the various operations. Extreme climatic conditions at high latitudes represent a serious challenge to vessels as well as to offshore infrastructure. Natural disasters and technological accidents, including oil spills, are likely to represent significant threats to the vulnerable Arctic natural environment and human life. In the harsh Arctic conditions, the military may be the only institution that possesses the necessary resources and is capable of providing safety and security on behalf of the various activities and operations.[84]

Therefore, along with a stronger presence of coast guards, border guards, and similar agencies, we may observe an expanding presence of naval forces as the economic activities improve. Nevertheless, as in the case of Arctic energy extraction and transpolar shipping, this scenario belongs to the future. As estimated by U.S. Navy Chief of Naval Operations Admiral Gary Roughead, routine military presence in the Arctic is not expected before 2025.[85]

However, an increasing military presence in the region, even if not intended primarily for power projection, is a sensitive issue. Despite the pragmatism and ongoing cooperation in the Arctic region, mistrust—the Cold War's legacy—is not entirely gone and may be easy to fuel. On various occasions, Russian political and military authorities have touched on the prevailing sense of insecurity vis-à-vis other actors' military presence in the region, particularly that of the United States and NATO, which are traditionally seen as potential adversaries of Russia and suspected of having anti-Russian strategic agendas.[86] A strengthening military presence by the individual Arctic littoral states, all members of NATO, may be viewed instead as an Alliance initiative in the region and thus considered to be a security problem. This suspicion has been repeatedly voiced by Russia's authorities.[87]

One of the main concerns in Russian security and defense considerations has been the emergence of stronger military powers on the country's borders, the Arctic included. In the preliminary Russian assessments of the transformation of the Arctic as a theater of maritime operations, the emphasis has been on challenges rather than opportunities deriving from it. During the Cold War, the Arctic Ocean was considered an operational front primarily for launching and flight routes of nuclear missiles. Surface vessel deployment by both the United States and the Soviet Union in the Arctic Ocean was difficult because of ice cover and was thus limited. But the expected opening of the Arctic may increase the inclination of foreign naval elements toward Arctic deployments.[88]

There has been concern in Russia that such a scenario may negatively affect the country's security, with a strengthened naval presence and power projection by other states in the polar maritime zone close to Russian borders.[89] Representatives of the Russian military and administration have expressed their dissatisfaction with the international focus on "hard" security in the region and warned against "attempts of the region's militarisation."[90]

Russia plays an important role in the strategies and policies of all the other Arctic actors. As argued above, much of the interest in the Arctic has been generated by Russia's increased military activity in the region, initially combined with an assertive anti-Western rhetoric. In 2007 there were more flights by Russian Long Range Aviation (LRA) than in the entire period from 1991 to 2006. The number of flights slightly increased in 2008 and has continued since at the same level. The economic crisis has thus not affected the military activity, unless it was planned to be boosted further. Air activity, exercised mainly by strategic bombers and support aircraft along the western, northern, and eastern routes into the North Atlantic, Arctic, and Pacific Oceans, has rehearsed basically the same missions as during the Cold War.

Russian naval activity has also been on the rise, including several high-profile naval exercises and more patrols by strategic and attack submarines. The exercises and maneuvers show that the Russian armed forces in the High North[91] are today better prepared to participate in more complex air and maritime operations than a few years ago. Nevertheless, the increased military activity is impressive only if compared to the long period of stagnation and decay in the Russian armed forces after the collapse of the Soviet Union and is far below the average Cold War levels.

Many commentators and experts have interpreted Russia's intensified military presence as an expression of the country's Arctic ambitions. However, the increased activity has been primarily a part of Russia's broader military strategy, often transiting the Arctic air and maritime domains, but in most cases not directed explicitly at them.

Despite the near collapse of important sectors of the Russian military since the 1990s, the Arctic has maintained a prominent place in Russia's strategic military thinking, in particular in the country's deterrence strategy as an important basing and operational area for the sea-based nuclear forces deployed with the Northern Fleet. The nuclear deterrent is still a key element of Russian defense policy, essential to uphold the country's great power status by compensating for the country's weakness in conventional forces. For those reasons, maintaining and upgrading the nuclear capabilities have been given the highest priority in military modernization efforts.

The Northern Fleet has been based in the region due to a number of conditions that make the area well-suited to strategic naval operations. Among them are direct and easy access to the Atlantic Ocean and the Arctic, manageable ice conditions, and close proximity to potential targets. There is also a range of important elements of defense industry and infrastructure, such as shipyards, intelligence installations, and the Plesetsk Cosmodrome launch site for military satellites and intercontinental ballistic missiles. The military relevance of the High North has been strengthened by the geopolitical changes after the dissolution of the Soviet Union, which limited Russia's access to the Baltic and the Black Seas.[92]

Apart from the LRA, Russia's strategic nuclear submarines (SSBN) are another essential part of the nuclear triad. Russia has almost completed modernization of the older nuclear component, the six *Delta IV* class submarines deployed with the Northern Fleet, in addition to the *Typhoon* class SSBN, currently used as a platform for testing the new generation missile, the Bulava.[93] The focus on maintaining nuclear strike

113

capability has been expressed in the priority given to building three fourth-generation *Borei* (*Dolgoruky*) class submarines. Russia faces serious challenges in developing the new missile and is struggling with delays in the construction. These problems make the announced plan of building eight *Borei* submarines by 2015 too optimistic.[94] However, the leadership is determined to continue work on the project, since there is no alternative to it.[95]

Russia's highly publicized plans to significantly strengthen naval assets capable of global reach are partly an expression of the country's foreign policy ambitions as driven by a vision of its rightful place among what has been perceived as a few independent centers of power and influence in global affairs. These plans have not been directly connected with developments in the Arctic, although their implementation will have an impact on the regional strategic environment there. As in many aspects of Russia's policies, however, there is a wide gap between ambitions and realities. The naval buildup will be limited by economic constraints as well as structural problems within the Russian military-industrial complex, and its success depends on the leadership's ability to turn the widely publicized economic modernization program into reality.

Russia's leadership underlines the necessity to maintain a credible military force in the North, capable of providing security under various scenarios touching the military and political situation in the region.[96] Particular challenges are related to surveillance and protection of the nearly 20,000 kilometer Russian state border along the ice-reduced Arctic Ocean.[97] According to the Arctic policy statement, the economic development and potential increased human activity will require reinforcements of the FSB border guard units. The growing importance of activities in the Arctic of Russia, as well as the increasing interest of other players, may be generating new tasks and thus new driving forces for the various security structures in the region, including the Russian Navy. As economic activities take off, we may expect further increases.

CONCLUSIONS

The Arctic remains one of the most peaceful regions on the world map, as well as one of Russia's most stable borderlands. Simultaneously, it is a resource-rich region with the potential to become a new strategically important channel of maritime communications. The commercial viability of the Arctic and potential sharp increase in economic activities are, however, a rather long-term eventuality and will depend on a number of factors. Nevertheless, despite the existing uncertainties, the Arctic potential alone continues to attract the attention of many key players, inciting them to respond to the evolving policies of each other.

Much of the focus on the Arctic worldwide has been generated by alarming expectations with regard to how churlish the major actors can behave when presented with such extraordinary economic opportunities. Although the unresolved jurisdictional issues involve some degree of uncertainty, the likelihood of use of military force is not very strong, even if certain scenarios, including escalation of an unintended incident under "perfect storm" conditions, cannot be fully discounted. While much of the alarmist rhetoric lacks a foundation in reality, there is still the risk of increased tensions in interstate relations deriving from the coexisting diverging interests. The military presence of various actors in the Arctic, a prospect that may be enhanced by climatic warming, may be one of such problematic issues. Transparency, inclusiveness, and dialogue will be needed in order to manage these developments without provoking mutual suspicions of the parties' motives and escalation of mutual fears.

Russia holds the key to political development in the region. The Arctic, particularly the High North, is of strong economic and military significance to Russia. The country's geopolitical position gives it a unique potential to influence many of the economic activities in the Arctic in the future, particularly regarding energy extraction and maritime transport along the NSR. At the same time, Russia is the strongest military power in the Arctic. The region plays an important role in the country's broader military strategy, particularly in nuclear deterrence, and is thus likely to remain of high importance to Russia in the foreseeable future.

The near complete dependence of the Russian economy on oil and gas is one the main driving forces for Russia's stronger engagement in the region. However, the ambitious economic development plan envisaging a variety of commercial and industrial initiatives has been suffering from the effects of the global crisis, unfavorable dynamics on energy markets, and structural problems within the Russian economy. As recent developments have shown, the economic slump may strengthen pragmatism, cooperation, and incentives for liberalization in some areas of Russia's economic and foreign policies.[98] Nonetheless, at this stage of development of the country's economic and political houses, there is still a degree of uncertainty about Russia's possible future choices and thus its viability as a reliable partner. International cooperation in the Arctic at all levels can contribute to a reduction of this questioning.

The uncertainty about the direction in which developments in the Arctic will unfold and, as a result, about the precise nature of the challenges and threats deriving from it, justifies the increased attention of the international community toward the region. The unlikelihood that an economic boom and, in consequence, a sharp increase in government and business activity in the Arctic will occur in the immediate or near-term future gives the actors time to limit risks and do the necessary contingency planning to ensure tolerable outcomes. To meet requirements for operations in the Arctic, it will be necessary to enhance situational awareness, improve climatic forecasting, and conduct comprehensive mapping surveys, as well as to develop expertise in search and rescue, humanitarian assistance, and disaster response. Cooperation in meeting these challenges, while mitigating immediate conflicts of interests, can be the best way to strengthen existing and foster new patterns of international teamwork because it facilitates a common approach to security challenges in the region.[99] International cooperation, primarily regional, may not only be desirable, but, indeed, it may be the sole option in meeting challenges emerging in the vast and evolving Arctic security environment, with its still many unforeseen scenarios and consequences.

REFERENCES

Agreement between the United States of America and the Union of Soviet Socialist Republics on the Maritime Boundary, June 1, 1990, New York: United Nations, Maritime Space: Maritime Zones and Maritime Delimitation, available from *www.un.org/Depts/los/LEGISLATIONANDTREATIES/PDFFILES/TREATIES/USA-RUS1990MB.PDF*.

Akimoto, Kazumine, *Power Games in the Arctic Ocean*, Tokyo, Japan: Ocean Policy Research Foundation, English summary of an article which appeared in the OPRF's *Arctic Ocean Quarterly*, summer 2009, published in Japanese.

Arctic Security: New Great Game? Panel Discussion at the Halifax International Security Forum 2009, German Marshall Sound, Halifax, Nova Scotia, Canada, November 21, 2009.

"Atomflot" rasschityvaet chto novye ledokoly nachnut stroit v 2011 godu," *RIA novosti*, October 17, 2009.

Bacon, Lance M., "Ice breaker," *Armed Forces Journal*, March 2010, available from *www.afji.com/features/*.

Balyberdin, Alexander, "Arctic in the system of priorities for maritime activities," *Military Parade*, No. 4, 2009.

Bochkarev, Danila, "Energy diversification towards the East—strategic imperative and operational response to the uncertainty of energy demand," *Baltic Rim Economies*, Issue No. 1, February 19, 2010.

Brigham, Lawson W., "Navigating the New Maritime Arctic," *USNI Naval Review*, May 2009.

Brubaker, R. Douglas, and Willy Østreng, "The Northern Sea Route Regime: Exquisite Superpower Subterfuge?" *Ocean Development & International Law*, October–December 99, Vol. 30, Issue 4, 1999.

Bruusgaard, Kristin Ven, "Fiskerikonflikter i Barentshavet—potensial for eskelaring? En komparativ studie av russiske reaksjonsmønstre under oppbringelsen av "Tsjernigov," 2001, og "Elektron," 2005," *FFI Raport*, Kjeller, 2006/03167.

Canada's Northern Strategy: Our North, Our Heritage, Our Future, published under the authority of the Minister of Indian Affairs and Northern Development and Federal Interlocutor for Métis and Non-Status Indians, Ottawa, Canada, available from *www.northernstrategy.ca/cns/cns-eng.asp#chp3*.

Circum-Arctic Resource Appraisal: Estimates of Undiscovered Oil and Gas North of the Arctic Circle, U.S. Geological Survey Fact Sheet July 2008, available from *energy.usgs.gov/arctic*.

Communication from the Commission to the European Parliament and the Council, "The European Union and the Arctic," COM (2008) 763 Final, Brussels, Belgium, November 20, 2008, available from *ec.europa.eu*.

De Hoop, Scheffer Jaap, Speech on security prospects in the High North, available from *www.nato.int/cps/en/SID-C3FDF602-F35F2667/natolive/opinions_50077.htm*.

Denmark: Arktis i en brydningstid. Forslag til strategi for aktiviteter i det arktiske område, May 2008, available from *www.um.dk/NR/rdonlyres/962AFDC2-30CE-412D-B7C7-070241C7D9D8/0/ARKTISK_STRATEGI.pdf*.

Diesen, Sverre, Norwegian Chief of Defence, "New Perspectives on Military Power in the Arctic," Kjetil Skogrand, ed., *Emerging from the Frost: Security in the 21st Century Arctic*, Oslo, Norway: Oslo Files on Defence and Security, February 2008.

"Eight Borei-class subs to be commissioned under state arms program 2007-2015," *Itar-Tass*, March 23, 2010.

Energeticheskaya strategiya Rossii na period do 2030 goda, November 2009, available from *www.energystrategy.ru*.

Europe's Northern Security Dimension, Document C/2016, European Security and Defence Assembly, Assembly of Western European Union, 55th Sess., November 5, 2008, accepted by the Assembly on December 4, 2008, available from *www.assembly-weu.org/en/presse/cp/2008/43-2008.php*.

European Parliament (EP) Resolution on Arctic governance of October 9, 2008, available from *www.europarl.europa.eu/sides/getDoc. do?type=TA&language=EN&reference=P6-TA-2008-0474.*

Foreign Affairs, Council on Foreign Relations, March/April 2008.

Gaaze, Konstantin, and Mikhail Zygar, "Pust' opyat; budet solntse," *Russkii Newsweek*, May 9, 2010.

"Gazprom resolves to postpone Bovanenkovo field commissioning," *Scandinavia Gas and Oil Magazine*, June 22, 2009, available from *www.scandoil.com/moxie-bm2/news/gazprom-resolves-to-postpone-bovanenkovo-field-com.shtml.*

"German ships sailing through North East Passage," *Telegraph*, September 11, 2009.

Howard, Roger, *The Arctic Gold Rush: The New Race for Tomorrow's Natural Resources*, London, UK: Continuum, 2009.

Internal sea waters, territorial sea and adjacent zone of the Russian Federation, July 31, 1998, State Duma of the Russian Federation, available from *wbase.duma.gov.ru.*

Intergovernmental Panel on Climate Change, *Fourth Assessment Report*, 2007, available from *www.ipcc.ch.*

Interview with Alexei Moskovsky, General, Commander of Armament and Deputy Defense Minister, "On condition of the Navy," *Security&Defence, WPS Agency Bulletin*, Moscow, March 3, 2008.

Interview with Sergei Ivanov, Deputy Prime Minister, *Rossiiskaya gazeta*, March 30, 2010.

Interview with Vladimir Vysotskii, Commander-in-Chief of the Russian Navy, "The Navy should reflect the national interests and economic potential of our country," *Moscow Defense Brief*, January 2010.

Interview with Vladimir Vysotskii, Commander-in-Chief of the Russian Navy, *RIA novosti*, July 26, 2009.

Interview with Yurii Trutnev, Minister for Natural Resources and Ecology, "Teplo, eshcho teplee," *Rossiiskaya gazeta*, January 11, 2010.

Jakobson, Linda, "China prepares for an ice-free Arctic," *SIPRI Insights on Peace and Security*, No. 2010/2, March 2010, Stockholm International Peace Research Institute.

Jensen, Øystein, and Svein Vigeland Rottem, "The politics of security and international law in Norway's Arctic waters," *Polar Record*, Vol. 46, 2009, No. 236, 2010, pp. 75–83.

Johannessen, Ola M., and Lasse H. Pettersson, "Arctic Climate and Shipping," Rose Gottemoeller and Rolf Tamnes, eds., *High North High Stakes: Security, Energy, Transport, Environment*, Bergen, Norway: Fagbokforlaget, 2008.

Joint Statement on maritime delimitation and cooperation in the Barents Sea and the Arctic Ocean, Oslo, Norway, March 27, 2010, available from *www.regjeringen.no/upload/UD/Vedlegg/Folkerett/030427 _english_4.pdf*.

Jørgensen, Jørgen Holten, *Russisk Svalbard-politikk. Eksterne og interne forklaringsfaktorer*, Hovedoppgave, Norway: Institutt for statsvitenskap, Universitetet i Oslo, September 2003.

"Kirienko otsenil atomnyi ledokol 3–go pokoleniya na 17 mlrd rublei," *Rosbalt Biznes*, April 21, 2009, available from *www. rosbalt.ru*.

Klimaticheskaya doktrina Rossiiskoi Federatsii, December 17, 2009, available from *www.kremlin.ru/news/6365*.

Kontseptsiya dolgostrochnogo sotsialno-ekonomicheskogo razvitiya Rossiiskoi Federatsii na period do 2020 goda, Moscow, Russia: Ministry for Economic Development and Trade, November 17, 2008, available from *www.government.ru*.

Kovalev, Vladimir, "Russia talks up Arctic claims," *Former Soviet Union Oil & Gas Monitor*, March 24, 2010, Week 11.

Lasserre, Frédéric, "High North Shipping. Myths and Realities," Sven G. Holtsmark and Brooke A. Smith-Windsor, eds., *Security Prospects in the High North. Geostrategic Thaw or Freeze?* Forum Paper No. 7, May 2009, Rome, Italy: NATO Defense College, available from *www.ndc.nato.int/download/downloads.php?icode=80*.

Lawson, W. Brigham, "Thinking About the Arctic's Future: Scenarios for 2040," *The Futurist*, September–October 2007.

"Lavrov surprised by NATO exercise," *Barents Observer*, March 25, 2009.

Lundestad, Ingrid, "Will the United States become more active in the Arctic?," March 12, 2010, available from *Atlantic-Community.org*.

Makarov, Nikolai, Chief of the General Staff, "Rossiiskii VMF siadet na khvost korabiami NATO v Arktike," *Izvestiya*, February 24, 2009.

Mäkinen, Hanna, "Shale gas—a game changer in the global energy play?" *Baltic Rim Economies*, Issue No. 1, February 19, 2010.

Malkova, Irina, "Gazprom tianet vremia," *Vedomosti*, July 22, 2009.

Marine Shipping Assessment 2009 Report, available from *www.pame.is/amsa/amsa-2009-report*.

Maslowski, Wieslaw, "Beyond Zero Emissions," March 24, 2008, available from *beyondzeroemissions.org/media/radio/dr-wieslaw-maslowski-predicted-2013-ice-free-summer-arctic-five-years-ago-now-he-says-ma*.

Medvedev, Dmitrii, *Speech at Meeting of the Russian Security Council on Protecting Russia's National Interests in the Arctic*, September 17, 2008, available from *eng.kremlin.ru*.

Mejlænder-Larsen, and Espeland Øyvind Morten, *Arctic Container Project*, Det Norske Veritas, September 1, 2009.

"Minenergo FR gotovo obsuzhdat' s chastnymi neftekompaniyami predlozheniya po shel'fu," *Neft' Rossii*, April 21, 2010, available from *www.oilru.com/news/173985*.

"Na shel'fe, krome "Rosnefti," dolzhny rabotat' i drugie kompanii—MPR," *RIA novosti*, March 30, 2010.

"Neftegazovye okmpanii sokratili investitsii v geologorazvedku na 20-30%, *Arkhangel'skie novosti*, September 2, 2009.

New Building Blocks in the North, The Norwegian Government, April 2009, available from *www.regjeringen.no/en*.

O vniesenii izmenenii v nekotorye zakonodatel'nye akty Rossiiskoi Federatsii v chasti Gosudarstvennogo regulirovaniya torgovogo moreplavaniya po trassam v akvatorii Severnogo morskogo puti, March 15, 2010, available from *www.mintrans.ru/pressa/zakon_mrt/proekt/fz_smp_14 .doc*.

Offerdal, Kristine, "High North Energy: Myths and Realities," Sven G. Holtsmark and Brooke A. Smith-Windsor, eds., *Security Prospects in the High North: Geostrategic Thaw or Freeze?* Forum Paper No. 7, May 2009, Rome, Italy; NATO Defense College, available from *www.ndc.nato.int/download/downloads.php?icode=80*.

Osnovy gosudarstvennoi politiki Rossiiskoi Federatsii v Arktike, The Government of the Russian Federation, Moscow, Russia, June 14, 2001, *www.arcticregion.ru/region/economics/469.html*.

Osnovy gosudarstvennoi politiki Rossiiskoi Federatsii v Arktike na period do 2020 goda i dalneishuyu perspektivu, Moscow, Russia: Security Council of the Russian Federation, September 18, 2008, available from *www.scrf.gov.ru*.

Outer limits of the continental shelf beyond 200 nautical miles from the baselines: Submissions to the Commission: Submission by the Russian Federation, available from *www.un.org*.

Øverland, Indra, "The surge in unconventional gas — implications for Russian export strategies," *Baltic Rim Economies*, Issue No. 1, February 19, 2010.

Press release, Meeting between Prime Minister Vladimir Putin and Sergei Kirienko, October 16, 2008, available from *www.government.ru*.

Press release, Security Council of the Russian Federation, March 27, 2009, available from *www.scrf.gov.ru/news/421.html*.

Press release, Security Council of the Russian Federation, September 13, 2008, available from *www.scrf.gov.ru*.

Press release 056/2010, Government Communications Unit, Finland, February 17, 2010, available from *www.valtioneuvosto.fi/ajankohtaista/tiedotteet/tiedote/en.jsp?oid=288128*.

Ragner, Claes Lykke, "Den norra sjövägen" ("The Northern Sea Route"), Torsten Hallberg, ed., *Barents — ett gränsland i Norden*, Stockholm, Sweden: Arena Norden, 2008, available from *www.fni.no*.

Remarks by Russian Minister of Foreign Affairs Sergey Lavrov at Arctic Council Session, Tromsø, April 29, 2009, Ministry of Foreign Affairs of the Russian Federation, available from *www.ln.mid.ru*.

"RF iz-za otsrochki Shtokmana poteryala rynok gaza v SShA — MPR," *Ria novosti*, March 30, 2010.

"Russia could lose its nuclear icebreaker fleet in 2016-2017 — Atomflot," *Interfax*, October 2009.

"Russia warns against militarisation of Arcitc," *Barents Observer*, July 23, 2009, *Russian Strategic Nuclear Forces*, available from *russianforces.org/*.

Shtokman Gas Condensate Deposit Barents Sea, Russia, available from *www.offshore-technology.com/projects/shtokman*.

Statement by the Russian Foreign Ministry (MFA) spokesman, Andrei Nesterenko, Moscow, Russia, *Murman News*, July 27, 2009.

Stigset, Marianne, "BP Oil Spill May Thwart Industry Push Into Norwegian Arctic," May 11, 2010, available from *Bloomberg.com.*

Strategiya izucheniya i osvoeniya neftegazovogo potentsiala kontinentalnogo shelfa Rossiiskoi Federatsii na period do 2020 goda — proekt, Moscow, Russia: Ministry of Natural Resources of the Russian Federation, September 2008, available from *www.rsppenergy.ru.*

Strategiya natsionalnoi bezopasnosti Rossiiskoi Federatsii do 2020 goda, May 12, 2009, available from *www.scrf.gov.ru/documents/99.html.*

The Arctic Climate Impact Assessment, available from *www.acia.uaf.edu.*

"The Arctic is no place for military blocs," *Voice of Russia*, October 15, 2009.

The Danish Defence Agreement, 2010–2014, The Danish Parliament, June 24, 2009, available from *www.fmn.dk.*

The Ilulissat Declaration, May 28, 2008, available from *www.um.dk.*

The National Security Presidential Directive and Homeland Security Presidential Directive, Arctic Region Policy, Washington, DC: The White House, January 9, 2009, available from *georgewbush-whitehouse.archives.gov.*

The Norwegian Government's Strategy for the High North, December 2006, available from *www.regjeringen.no/en.*

Transportnaya strategiya Rossiiskoi Federatsii na period do 2030 goda, Ministry of Transport of the Russian Federation, November 22, 2008, available from *www.mintrans.ru.*

Treaty between Norway, The United States of America, Denmark, France, Italy, Japan, the Netherlands, Great Britain and Ireland and the British overseas Dominions and Sweden concerning Spitsbergen signed in Paris 9th February 1920, available from *www.sysselmannen.no/hovedEnkel.aspx?m=45301.*

"Trutnev: Nekotorye vedomstva na soglasny s liberalizatsiei dostupa k neftyanym mestorozhdeniyam na shel'fe RF," *Neft' Rossii*, April 20, 2010, available from *www.oilru.com/news/173740*.

US Geological Survey's World Petroleum Assessment 2000-Description and Results, available from *pubs.usgs.gov/dds/dds-060/*.

"V Rossii gotovitsya zakon o Severnom morskom puti," February 12, 2009, *Regnum.ru*.

Zysk, Katarzyna, "Russia and the High North: Security and Defence Perspectives," Sven G. Holtsmark and Brooke A. Smith-Windsor, eds., *Security Prospects in the High North: Geostrategic Thaw or Freeze?* Forum Paper No. 7, May 2009, Rome, Italy: NATO Defense College, available from *www.ndc.nato.int/download/publications/fp_07.pdf*.

Zysk, Katarzyna, "Russia's Arctic Strategy: Ambitions and Constraints," *Joint Force Quarterly*, Issue 57, 2nd Quarter 2010, Washington, DC: National Defense University Press, available from *www.ndu.edu/press/jfq_pages/editions/i57/zysk.pdf*.

ENDNOTES - CHAPTER 4

1. This chapter was written as part of the Geopolitics in the High North research program (*www.geopoliticsnorth.org*). The author is grateful for useful comments on earlier drafts of this paper from Paal Sigurd Hilde, Sven G. Holtsmark, and Kristine Offerdal.

2. The term "Arctic" as used herein pertains to all areas north of the Arctic Circle.

3. See, for instance, *Foreign Affairs*, March/April 2008; *European Parliament (EP) Resolution on Arctic Governance* of October 9, 2008, talked among other things about "the ongoing race for the natural resources in the Arctic." The document is available from the EP's official homepage, *www.europarl.europa.eu/sides/getDoc.do ?type=TA&language=EN&reference=P6-TA-2008-0474*.

4. See the *Joint Statement on maritime delimitation and cooperation in the Barents Sea and the Arctic Ocean*, signed by President Dmitrii Medvedev and Foreign Minister Jonas Gahr Støre in Oslo, Norway, on March 27, 2010, *www.regjeringen.no/upload/UD/ Vedlegg/Folkerett/030427_english_4.pdf*.

5. *Osnovy gosudarstvennoi politiki Rossiiskoi Federatsii v Arktike na period do 2020 goda i dalneishuyu perspektivu*, September 18, 2008, Moscow, Russia: Security Council of the Russian Federation, available from *www.scrf.gov.ru* (hereafter *Osnovy*, 2008); Dmitrii Medvedev, *Speech at Meeting of the Russian Security Council on Protecting Russia's National Interests in the Arctic*, September 17, 2008, available from *eng.kremlin.ru*; Press release, Security Council of the Russian Federation, September 13, 2008, available from *www. scrf.gov.ru*.

6. This assessment included, among other things, some of the Arctic areas, *US Geological Survey's World Petroleum Assessment 2000 — Description and Results*, available from *pubs.usgs.gov/dds/ dds-060/*. The first energy estimate focused explicitly on the Arctic was made in 2008: *Circum-Arctic Resource Appraisal: Estimates of Undiscovered Oil and Gas North of the Arctic Circle*, U.S. Geological Survey Fact Sheet July 2008, available from *energy.usgs.gov/arctic*.

See also Kristine Offerdal, "High North Energy. Myths and Realities," Sven G. Holtsmark and Brooke A. Smith-Windsor, eds., *Security Prospects in the High North. Geostrategic Thaw or Freeze?* Forum Paper No. 7, May 2009, Rome, Italy: NATO Defense College, p. 156, available from *www.ndc.nato.int/download/downloads.php?icode=80.*

7. Offerdal, p. 153.

8. Roger Howard, *The Arctic Gold Rush: The New Race for Tomorrow's Natural Resources*, London, UK: Continuum, 2009.

9. Lawson W. Brigham, "Thinking About the Arctic's Future. Scenarios for 2040," *The Futurist*, September–October 2007.

10. Ola M. Johannessen and Lasse H. Pettersson, "Arctic Climate and Shipping," Rose Gottemoeller and Rolf Tamnes, eds., *High North High Stakes: Security, Energy, Transport, Environment*, Bergen, Norway: Fagbokforlaget, 2008, p. 95.

11. The 2004 report from the *Arctic Climate Impact Assessment* (ACIA) predicted a dramatic reduction in September ice coverage in the Arctic, normally the annual minimum, in this century. However, later the assessment proved too optimistic. The ACIA's report is available from *www.acia.uaf.edu.*

12. Johannessen and Pettersson, pp. 96–97.

13. Intergovernmental Panel on Climate Change, *Fourth Assessment Report*, 2007, available from *www.ipcc.ch.*

14. Among other things, according to the expert in Arctic oceanography, Dr. Wieslaw Maslowski. See transcription of interview with Dr. Maslowski: "Beyond Zero Emissions," March 24, 2008, available from *beyondzeroemissions.org/media/radio/dr-wieslaw-maslowski-predicted-2013-ice-free-summer-arctic-five-years-ago-now-he-says-ma.*

15. The term "High North" as used in this paper refers to the Barents Sea, the Norwegian Sea, and the southern parts of the Polar Sea. This region is also called the European Arctic.

16. *The Norwegian Government's Strategy for the High North*, December 2006, available from *www.regjeringen.no/en*. The Strategy was updated in 2009, but the main goals of the policy remained the same. See *New Building Blocks in the North*, The Norwegian Government, April 2009, available from *www.regjeringen.no/en*.

17. *Osnovy*, 2008. Elements of the Russian Arctic policy have been analyzed in Katarzyna Zysk, "Russia's Arctic Strategy: Ambitions and Constraints," *Joint Force Quarterly*, Issue 57, 2nd Quarter 2010, Washington, DC: National Defense University Press, available from *www.ndu.edu/press/jfq_pages/editions/i57/zysk.pdf*. The previous fundamentals of the Arctic policy were adopted by the Russian government in 2001. See *Osnovy gosudarstvennoi politiki Rossiiskoi Federatsii v Arktike*, Moscow, Russia: The Government of the Russian Federation, June 14, 2001, available from *www.arcticregion.ru/region/economics/469.html* (hereafter *Osnovy*, 2001).

18. Denmark drafted a preliminary Arctic document in May 2008, while in February 2010 the Finnish Prime Minister's Office appointed a working group to prepare a report on Finland's policy for the region. See *Denmark: Arktis i en brydningstid. Forslag til strategi for aktiviteter i det arktiske område*, May 2008, available from *www.um.dk/NR/rdonlyres/962AFDC2-30CE-412D-B7C7-070241C7D9D8/0/ARKTISK_STRATEGI.pdf*; Press release 056/2010, Government Communications Unit, Finland, February 17, 2010, available from *www.valtioneuvosto.fi/ajankohtaista/tiedotteet/tiedote/en.jsp?oid=288128*.

19. *Canada's Northern Strategy: Our North, Our Heritage, Our Future*, The conservative government of Prime Minister Stephen Harper, Ottawa, Canada: Minister of Indian Affairs and Northern Development and Federal Interlocutor for Métis and Non-Status Indians, July 2009, available from *www.northernstrategy.ca/cns/cns-eng.asp#chp3*.

20. Ingrid Lundestad, "Will the United States become more active in the Arctic?" March 12, 2010, available from *Atlantic-Community.org*. The United States updated the 1994 policy directive on the Arctic in January 2009. See *The National Security Presidential Directive and Homeland Security Presidential Directive, Arctic region policy*, Washington, DC: The White House, January 9, 2009, available from *georgewbush-whitehouse.archives.gov*.

21. *Europe's Northern Security Dimension*, Document C/2016, European Security and Defence Assembly, Assembly of Western European Union, 55th Sess., November 5, 2008. The report was accepted by the Assembly on December 4, 2008, and is available from *www.assembly-weu.org/en/presse/cp/2008/43-2008.php*.

22. The Seminar on *Security Prospects in the High North*, hosted by the Icelandic Government, took place in Reykjavik, Iceland, on January 28–29, 2009, reports available from *www.nato.int/cps/en/natolive/news_49745.htm*. A speech delivered at the meeting by NATO Secretary General Jaap de Hoop Scheffer is available from NATO's homepage, *www.nato.int/cps/en/SID-C3FDF602-F35F2667/natolive/opinions_50077.htm*; *Communication from the Commission to the European Parliament and the Council*, The European Union and the Arctic, COM (2008) 763 Final, Brussels, Belgium, November 20, 2008, available from *ec.europa.eu*. On December 8, 2009, the Foreign Affairs Council adopted guidelines for the future EU Arctic policy, available from *www.se2009.eu/en/meetings_news/2009/12/8/a_step_towards_an_eu_arctic_policy*. See also the aforementioned resolution of European Parliament on the Arctic, *The European Parliament Resolution on Arctic Governance*, October 9, 2008.

23. Linda Jakobson, "China prepares for an ice-free Arctic," *SIPRI Insights on Peace and Security*, No. 2010/2, Stockholm, Sweden: Stockholm International Peace Research Institute, March 2010.

24. *Ibid*.

25. *Circum-Arctic Resource Appraisal*. For an analysis of prospects of development of Arctic offshore petroleum resources and their role in the global energy picture, see Offerdal.

26. *Circum-Arctic Resource Appraisal*; USGS Newsroom, July 23, 2008, available from *www.usgs.gov/newsroom*. The total amount of undiscovered conventional oil and gas resources in the Arctic is estimated to be approximately 90 billion barrels of oil, 1,669 trillion cubic feet of natural gas, and 44 billion barrels of natural gas liquids.

27. *Osnovy*, 2001; Strategiya izucheniya i osvoeniya neftega-zovogo potentsiala kontinentalnogo shelfa Rossiiskoi Federatsii na period do 2020 goda—proekt, Moscow, Russia: Ministry of Natural Resources of the Russian Federation, September 2008, available from *www.rsppenergy.ru*.

28. Medvedev; Press release, Security Council of the Russian Federation, September 13, 2008.

29. *Osnovy*, 2008.

30. *Energeticheskaya strategiya Rossii na period do 2030 goda*, November 2009 available from *www.energystrategy.ru*.

31. *Osnovy*, 2008.

32. *Klimaticheskaya doktrina Rossiiskoi Federatsii*, December 17, 2009, in Russian, available from *www.kremlin.ru/news/6365*.

33. *Ibid.*

34. *Ibid.* See also an interview with Minister for Natural Resources and Ecology Yurii Trutnev, "Teplo, eshcho teplee," *Rossiiskaya gazeta*, January 11, 2010.

35. See, for instance, Marianne Stigset, "BP Oil Spill May Thwart Industry Push Into Norwegian Arctic," *Bloomberg.com*, May 11, 2010.

36. Reserves of gas in Shtokman have been put at 3.2 trillion cubic meters and 31 million tons of gas condensate. See *Shtokman Gas Condensate Deposit Barents Sea, Russia*, available from *www.offshore-technology.com/projects/shtokman*.

37. Irina Malkova, "Gazprom tianet vremia," *Vedomosti*, July 22, 2009.

38. "Gazprom resolves to postpone Bovanenkovo field commissioning," *Scandinavia Gas and Oil Magzine*, June 22, 2009, available from *www.scandoil.com/moxie-bm2/news/gazprom-resolves-to-postpone-bovanenkovo-field-com.shtml*.

39. Hanna Mäkinen, "Shale gas—a game changer in the global energy play?" *Baltic Rim Economies*, Issue No. 1, February 19, 2010, available from *www.tse.fi/FI/yksikot/erillislaitokset/pei/Documents/BRE2010/BRE_1_2010_Web.pdf.* On the same subject in this issue, see also Indra Øverland, "The surge in unconventional gas—implications for Russian export strategies"; and Danila Bochkarev, "Energy diversification towards the East—strategic imperative and operational response to the uncertainty of energy demand."

40. Mäkinen; Bochkarev.

41. *Ibid.*

42. Mäkinen.

43. "RF iz-za otsrochki Shtokmana poteryala rynok gaza v SShA—MPR," *Ria novosti*, March 30, 2010.

44. Interview with Deputy Prime Minister Sergei Ivanov, *Rossiiskaya gazeta*, March 30, 2010.

45. "Neftegazovye okmpanii sokratili investitsii v geologorazvedku na 20-30%," *Arkhangel'skie novosti*, September 2, 2009; "Na shel'fe, krome 'Rosnefti,' dolzhny rabotat' i drugie kompanii—MPR," *RIA novosti*, March 30, 2010.

46. See, for instance, "Minenergo FR gotovo obsuzhdat' s chastnymi neftekompaniyami predlozheniya po shel'fu," *Neft' Rossii*, April 21, 2010, available from *www.oilru.com/news/173985*; "Na shel'fe, krome "Rosnefti," dolzhny rabotat' i drugie kompanii—MPR," *RIA novosti*, March 30, 2010.

47. "Trutnev: Nekotorye vedomstva na soglasny s liberalizatsiei dostupa k neftyanym mestorozhdeniyam na shel'fe RF," *Neft' Rossii*, April 20, 2010, available from *www.oilru.com/news/173740.*

48. "Recent Warming Reverses Long-Term Arctic Cooling," *Science*, Vol. 325, No. 5945, September 4, 2009, pp. 1236–1239.

49. "German ships sailing through North East Passage," *Telegraph*, September 11, 2009.

50. Panel Discussion at the Halifax International Security Forum 2009: *Arctic Security: New Great Game?* Halifax, Nova Scotia, Canada: German Marshall Fund, November 21, 2009.

51. Morten Mejlænder-Larsen and Øyvind Espeland, *Arctic Container Project*, Det Norske Veritas, September 1, 2009.

52. See in particular an analysis by Frédéric Lasserre, "High North Shipping: Myths and Realities," Sven G. Holtsmark and Brooke A. Smith-Windsor, eds., *Security Prospects in the High North: Geostrategic Thaw or Freeze?* Forum Paper No. 7, May 2009, Rome, Italy: NATO Defense College, pp. 179–199; Morten Mejlænder-Larsenand Øyvind Espeland, *Arctic Container Project*, Det Norske Veritas, September 1, 2009.

53. Lasserre, pp. 179–199.

54. A thorough study of the potential and challenges has been conducted by the Arctic Council's Protection of the Arctic Marine Environment (PAME) working group: *Marine Shipping Assessment 2009 Report*, available from *www.pame.is/amsa/amsa-2009-report*. See also Lawson W. Brigham, "Navigating the New Maritime Arctic," *USNI Naval Review*, May 2009.

55. The cost of insurance for ships sailing via the Gulf of Aden towards the Suez Canal reportedly increased 10 times between September 2008 and March 2009, Jacobsen, p. 5.

56. Stephen M. Carmel, Senior Vice President, Maritime Services, Maersk Line Ltd., Panel Discussion at the Halifax International Security Forum 2009: *Arctic Security: New Great Game?*

57. Claes Lykke Ragner, "The Northern Sea Route," Torsten Hallberg, ed., *Barents – ett gränsland i Norden*, Stockholm, Sweden: Arena Norden, 2008, available from *www.fni.no*. A bill regulating commercial shipping through the Northern Sea Route has been prepared by the Russian Ministry of Transport: *O vniesenii izmenenii v nekotorye zakonodatel'nye akty Rossiiskoi Federatsii v chasti Gosudarstvennogo regulirovaniya torgovogo moreplavaniya po trassam v akvatorii Severnogo morskogo puti*, March 15, 2010, available from *www.mintrans.ru/pressa/zakon_mrt/proekt/fz_smp_14.doc*.

58. *Kontseptsiya dolgostrochnogo sotsialno-ekonomicheskogo razvitiya Rossiiskoi Federatsii na period do 2020 goda*, Moscow, Russia: Ministry for Economic Development and Trade, November 17, 2008, available from *www.government.ru*. See also *Transportnaya strategiya Rossiiskoi Federatsii na period do 2030 godai*, Moscow, Russia: Ministry of Transport of the Russian Federation, November 22, 2008, available from *www.mintrans.ru*.

59. Ragner.

60. "First oil shipment planned for Northern Sea Route," *Barents Observer*, February 25, 2010, available from *www.barentsobserver.com/index.php?id=4752806&xxforceredir=1&noredir=1*.

61. Bochkarev.

62. As indicated in the Arctic policy document, *Osnovy*, 2008. Six of the seven active nuclear-powered icebreakers will approach the end of their service in 2020. "Russia could lose its nuclear icebreaker fleet in 2016-2017-Atomflot," *Interfax*, October 2009.

63. Press release from the meeting between Prime Minister Vladimir Putin and S. Kirienko, October 16, 2008, available from *www.government.ru*; "Kirienko otsenil atomnyi ledokol 3-go pokoleniya na 17 mlrd rublei," *Rosbalt Biznes*, April 21, 2009, available from *www.rosbalt.ru*; "'Atomflot' rasschityvaet chto novye ledokoly nachnut stroit v 2011 godu," *RIA novosti*, October 17, 2009.

64. See Offerdal.

65. *Circum-Arctic Resource Appraisal.*

66. *Outer limits of the continental shelf beyond 200 nautical miles from the baselines: Submissions to the Commission: Submission by the Russian Federation*, available from *www.un.org*.

67. *Osnovy*, 2008.

68. Quoted in Vladimir Kovalev, "Russia talks up Arctic claims," *Former Soviet Union Oil & Gas Monitor*, March 24, 2010, Week 11.

69. *Ibid.*

70. *Agreement between the United States of America and the Union of Soviet Socialist Republics on the Maritime Boundary,* June 1, 1990, United Nations, Maritime Space: Maritime Zones and Maritime Delimitation, available from *www.un.org/Depts/los/LEGISLA-TIONANDTREATIES/PDFFILES/TREATIES/USA-RUS1990MB.PDF.*

71. Two cases of a particularly difficult character, which took place in 2001 and 2005 in the Svalbard zone, have been described and analyzed by Kristin Ven Bruusgaard, "Fiskerikonflikter i Barentshavet—potensial for eskelaring? En komparativ studie av russiske reaksjonsmønstre under oppbringelsen av 'Tsjernigov' (2001) og 'Elektron' (2005)," *FFI Raport,* in Norwegian, Kjeller, 2006/03167.

72. *Treaty between Norway, The United States of America, Denmark, France, Italy, Japan, the Netherlands, Great Britain and Ireland and the British overseas Dominions and Sweden concerning Spitsbergen signed in Paris, 9th February 1920.* The text of the document is available from the home page of the Governor of Svalbard, *www.sysselmannen.no/hovedEnkel.aspx?m=45301.*

73. Jørgen Holten Jørgensen, *Russisk Svalbard-politikk. Eksterne og interne forklaringsfaktorer,* Hovedoppgave, Norway: Institutt for statsvitenskap, Universitetet i Oslo, September 2003, p. 89–91.

74. *Osnovy,* 2008. The NSR is regulated today by the law, "On Inner Sea Waters, Territorial Sea and Adjacent Zone of the Russian Federation," July 31, 1998, Moscow, Russia: State Duma of the Russian Federation. The Russian State Duma has been at work on drafting a federal law on the Northern Sea Route aimed at regulating shipping, determining external borders of the passage, and formalizing its legal status as Russia's national transport route. See "V Rossii gotovitsya zakon o Severnom morskom puti," *Regnum.ru,* February 12, 2009. *O vniesenii izmenenii v nekotorye zakonodatel'nye akty Rossiiskoi Federatsiii.*

75. "Internal sea waters, territorial sea and adjacent zone of the Russian Federation," Moscow, Russia: State Duma of the Russian Federation, July 31, 1998, available from *wbase.duma.gov.ru;*

A. L. Kolodkin and M. E. Volosov, "The Legal Regime of the Soviet Arctic: Major Issues," *Marine Policy*, Vol. 14, 1990, pp. 163–167, quoted in R. Douglas Brubaker and Willy Østreng, "The Northern Sea Route Regime: Exquisite Superpower Subterfuge?" *Ocean Development & International Law*, October–December 1999, Vol. 30, Issue 4, pp. 299–331; Ragner.

76. See an analysis by Øystein Jensen and Svein Vigeland Rottem, "The politics of security and international law in Norway's Arctic waters," *Polar Record*, Vol. 46, 2009, pp. 75–83.

77. As stated in *The Ilulissat Declaration*, May 28, 2008. The text of the declaration and supplementary information are available from the Danish Ministry of Foreign Affairs, *www.um.dk*.

78. See the Arctic policy document, as well as in the National Security Strategy, *Osnovy*, 2008; *Strategiya natsionalnoi bezopasnosti Rossiiskoi Federatsii do 2020 goda*, May 12, 2009, available from *www.scrf.gov.ru/documents/99.html*.

79. See *Remarks by Russian Minister of Foreign Affairs Sergey Lavrov at Arctic Council Session*, Tromsø, Norway: Ministry of Foreign Affairs of the Russian Federation, April 29, 2009, available from *www.ln.mid.ru*; Press release of the Security Council of the Russian Federation from March 27, 2009, available from *www.scrf.gov.ru/news/421.html*.

80. Panel Discussion at the Halifax International Security Forum 2009, *Arctic Security: New Great Game?*

81. *Ibid.*

82. As defined by George A. Backus and James H. Strickland, *Climate-Derived Tensions in Arctic Security*, SANDIA Report, SAND2008-6342, Sandia, NM: September 2008, pp. 11–12.

83. An interesting analysis of conflict potential in the region has been made by General Sverre Diesen, former Norwegian Chief of Defence, "New Perspectives on Military Power in the Arctic," Kjetil Skogrand, ed., *Emerging from the Frost: Security in the 21st Century Arctic*, Oslo, Norway: Oslo Files on Defence and Security, February 2008, pp. 89–101.

84. Panel Discussion at the Halifax International Security Forum 2009, *Arctic Security: New Great Game?*

85. Quoted in Lance M. Bacon, "Ice breaker," *Armed Forces Journal*, March 2010, available from *www.afji.com/features/*.

86. Russian perceptions of the NATO and U.S. military presence in the High North and the military strategic significance of the region to Russia are discussed in Katarzyna Zysk, "Russia and the High North: Security and Defence Perspectives," Sven G. Holtsmark and Brooke A. Smith-Windsor, eds., *Security Prospects in the High North: Geostrategic Thaw or Freeze?* Forum Paper No. 7, May 2009, Washington, DC: NATO Defense College, Rome, pp. 102–129, available from *www.ndc.nato.int/download/publications/fp_07.pdf*.

87. "The Arctic is no place for military blocs," *Voice of Russia*, October 15, 2009; "Russia warns against militarisation of Arcitc," *Barents Observer*, July 23, 2009; "Lavrov surprised by NATO exercise," *Barents Observer*, March 25, 2009.

88. Rear Admiral Kazumine Akimoto (Ret.), *Power Games in the Arctic Ocean*, Tokyo, Japan: Ocean Policy Research Foundation (OPRF), English summary of an article which appeared in the OPRF's *Arctic Ocean Quarterly*, Summer 2009 (in Japanese).

89. Vice-Admiral (Ret.) Alexander Balyberdin, "Arctic in the system of priorities for maritime activities," *Military Parade*, No. 4, 2009; "The Arctic is no place for military blocks," *Voice of Russia*, October 15, 2009, available from *ruvr.ru*; "Russia warns against militarization of Arctic," *Barents Observer*, July 23, 2009. The Russian authorities have also expressed discontent with the annual military exercises called Cold Response organized in Northern Norway with NATO member states. "Lavrov surprised by NATO exercise," *Barents Observer*, March 25, 2009.

90. See *The Danish Defence Agreement*, June 24, 2009, by the Danish Parliament, covering the period from 2010–14, pp. 9–10, available from *www.fmn.dk/eng/Defence%20Agreement/Pages/international operations.aspx*; a defense plan presented during election campaign by the currently in power Canadian Conservative Party, *Canadian American Strategic Review*, December 2005, available from *www.*

casr.ca/ft-harper1-1.htm. A statement by Chief of the General Staff General Nikolai Makarov, "Rossiiskii VMF siadet na khvost korabiami NATO v Arktike," *Izvestiya,* February 24, 2009. See also statements by Russian Foreign Ministry (MFA) spokesman Andrei Nesterenko, Moscow, Russia, *Murman News,* July 27, 2009, available from *www.murmannews.ru;* Balyberdin.

91. The term "High North" as used in this paper refers to the Barents Sea, the Norwegian Sea, and the southern parts of the Polar Sea. This region is also called the European Arctic.

92. The military strategic significance of the region to Russia has been analyzed in Zysk, "Russia and the High North," 2009.

93. For an overview of Russian strategic forces in Western sources, see *Russian Strategic nuclear Forces,* available from *russianforces.org/.*

94. Interview with CINC of the Russian Navy Admiral Vladimir Vysotskii, *RIA novosti,* July 26, 2009; General Alexei Moskovsky, Commander of Armament and Deputy Defense Minister of that time, "On condition of the Navy," *Security&Defence, WPS Agency Bulletin,* Moscow, Russia, March 3, 2008; "Eight Borei-class subs to be commissioned under state arms program 2007-2015," *Itar-Tass,* March 23, 2010.

95. Interview with Admiral Vladimir Vysotskii, Commander-in-Chief of the Russian Navy, "The Navy should reflect the national interests and economic potential of our country," *Moscow Defense Brief,* January 2010.

96. *Osnovy,* 2008.

97. The number is provided by the Russian Arctic document of 2001, *Osnovy,* 2001.

98. See the article concerning a new document in Russia's Foreign Ministry signaling a more pragmatic policy in relation to the West, Konstantin Gaaze and Mikhail Zygar', "Pust' opyat; budet solntse," *Russkii Newsweek,* May 9, 2010.

99. See interviews with Admiral Roughead and Rear Admiral David Titley in Bacon.

ABOUT THE CONTRIBUTORS

STEPHEN J. BLANK has served as the Strategic Studies Institute's resident expert on the Soviet bloc and the post-Soviet world since 1989. Prior to that he was Associate Professor of Soviet Studies at the Center for Aerospace Doctrine, Research, and Education, Maxwell Air Force Base, AL; and taught at the University of Texas, San Antonio, and at the University of California, Riverside. Dr. Blank is the editor of *Imperial Decline: Russia's Changing Position in Asia*, coeditor of the *Soviet Military and the Future*, and author of *The Sorcerer as Apprentice: Stalin's Commissariat of Nationalities, 1917-1924*. He has also written many articles and conference papers on Russia, the Commonwealth of Independent States, and Eastern European security issues. Dr. Blank's current research deals with proliferation, the revolution in military affairs, and energy and security in Eurasia. His two most recent books are *Russo-Chinese Energy Relations: Politics in Command*, London, UK: Global Markets Briefing, 2006; and *Natural Allies? Regional Security in Asia and Prospects for Indo-American Strategic Cooperation*, Carlisle, PA: Strategic Studies Institute, U.S. Army War College, 2005. Dr. Blank holds a B.A. in history from the University of Pennsylvania, and an M.A. and Ph.D. in history from the University of Chicago.

ARIEL COHEN is Senior Research Fellow in Russian and Eurasian Studies and International Energy Policy at the Katherine and Shelby Cullom Davis Institute for International Policy at The Heritage Foundation. Dr. Cohen is the author of *Russian Imperialism: Development and Crisis*.

ALEXANDR' GOLTS is the defense correspondent for *Yezhenedevnyi Zhurnal* (*Daily Journal*).

MARLÈNE LARUELLE is Senior Research Fellow with the Central Asia-Caucasus Institute & Silk Road Studies Program, and associated scholar at the Russian and Eurasian Department at Johns Hopkins University's School of Advanced International Studies, Washington, DC. Her main areas of expertise are nationalism, national identities, political philosophy, and the intellectual trends and geopolitical conceptions of Russian and Central Asian elites. She is an authority on Russian and Central Asian foreign policy think tanks and academia. Ms. Laruelle's English-language publications include *Russian Eurasianism: An Ideology of Empire* (Woodrow Wilson Press/Johns Hopkins University Press, 2008); *In the Name of the Nation: Nationalism and Politics in Contemporary Russia* (Palgrave, Spring 2009); and editor of *Russian Nationalism and the National Reassertion of Russia* (Routledge, Spring 2009).

KATARZYNA ZYSK is a Senior Fellow at the Department for International Security Policy at the Norwegian Institute for Defence Studies in Oslo. She has been a Visiting Research Scholar at the Center for Naval Warfare Studies/Strategic Research Department at the U.S. Naval War College, and a guest researcher at the University of Oslo. Dr. Zysk is a participant in the international research program *Geopolitics in the High North*, sponsored by the Norwegian Research Council with a post-doctoral research project on security developments in the Arctic focused on Russia's policies (2009–12). She is also associated with the research program, *The Emerging Arctic Security Environ-*

ment: External and Internal Dimensions, sponsored by the Network of Centres of Excellence of Canada. Her current research interests focus on strategic studies, security in the Arctic and international relations in the circumpolar region, Russian security and defense policy, particularly developments in the Russian Navy.

www.ingramcontent.com/pod-product-compliance
Lightning Source LLC
Chambersburg PA
CBHW080017280326
41934CB00015B/3382